Prentice-Hall, Inc., Englewood Cliffs, N. J.

# The

# Impact

# of

# Industry

WILBERT E. MOORE    Russell Sage Foundation

Library of Congress Catalog Card No.: 65-23228

Printed in the United States of America
C-45171(C)      C-45170(P)

Current printing (last digit):
11   10   9   8   7   6   5   4   3   2

This book is dedicated to
**SIMON KUZNETS**
Eminent scholar, good friend, and guiding
spirit in the analysis of economic change

PRENTICE-HALL INTERNATIONAL, INC.
London

PRENTICE-HALL OF AUSTRALIA, PTY., LTD.
Sydney

PRENTICE-HALL OF CANADA, LTD.
Toronto

PRENTICE-HALL OF INDIA (PRIVATE) LTD.
New Delhi

PRENTICE-HALL OF JAPAN, INC.
Tokyo

WILBERT E. MOORE / NEIL J. SMELSER    Editors

**Modernization of Traditional Societies Series**

The twentieth century will be called many
things by future historians—the Age of Global
War, perhaps, the Age of Mass Society,
the Age of the Psychoanalytic Revolution,
to name a few possibilities. One name that
historians certainly will not fail to give
our century is the Age of the New Nation. For,
evidently, the convulsive emergence of
the colonies into independence and their
subsequent struggle to join the ranks of the
prosperous, powerful, and peaceful is the
most remarkable revolution of our time.
Taking the world as a whole, men are now
preoccupied with no subject more than they
are with the travail of the New Nations.
The world of the social sciences
has been studying the pace of social
change in these newly emergent areas,
and from time to time has been engaging in
technical assistance and even in the giving
of advice on high levels of social strategy.
Little of this effort has reached publicly
accessible form. Though technical treatises
abound, and isolated, journalistic reports
of distinctly exotic countries are not
wanting, college curricula have scarcely
reflected either the scientific endeavors or
the world-wide revolutions in technology
and in political affairs.
This series on "Modernization of
Traditional Societies" is designed to
inform scholars, students, and citizens about
the way quiet places have come alive, and
to introduce at long last materials on

EDITORIAL      FOREWORD      the contemporary character of

developing areas into college curricula for the thought leaders of the near future. To these ends we have assembled experts over the range of the social sciences and over the range of the areas of the underdeveloped and newly developing sections of the earth that were once troublesome only to themselves.

We are proud to be participants in this series, and proud to offer each of its volumes to the literate world, with the hope that that world may increase, prosper, think, and decide wisely.

WILBERT E. MOORE
NEIL J. SMELSER

The modernization of traditional societies comes closer to being an all-encompassing process of social change than any other that history or the contemporary world offers. That is more particularly true because the component processes of change are not merely transitional; they persist in the advanced industrial societies. Not all of social dynamics, a ubiquitous feature of the human condition, is caught up in modernization, and it would be tediously trivial to relate everything to everything. But most of the large-scale structural changes in the modern world are indeed a part of the most profound, extensive, and enduring set of dynamic processes that mankind has yet experienced. Some of those changes are universally viewed as beneficent, and others, such as the capacity to end the whole charade quickly, can only be viewed by reasonably rational minds as providing unprecedented dangers.

Until the end of World War II there was little scholarly interest in the social transformation going on in the economically underdeveloped or newly developing areas. Some anthropologists, it is true, were turning their attention from the reconstruction of pristine tribal systems to the observation of such systems under the various kinds of external impact. A very few economists and sociologists, and even fewer political scientists, exhibited an interest in economic development and its non-economic concomitants.

PREFACE

No doubt a principal source of the more recent engagement of scholarly interest in "underdeveloped areas" has been external to the academic community, deriving rather from the demands for advice on social policy. Responsible governing officials in these areas have sought rapid economic transformation and have engaged in various official measures to achieve it. These measures have included obtaining "technical assistance" of several kinds and forms, both through the United Nations and its associated specialized agencies, and through national programs of assistance—for example, those of the metropolitan governments with respect to colonial or associated territories, and those of the "Point Four" and successor agencies of the United States government. For these programs, first economists, and then other social scientists, have been called upon to study and advise.

Some developments within the social sciences coincided with these practical concerns, and it would be unduly cynical to link those developments entirely to outside forces. With slow and faltering steps, the several social scientific fields have been moving from an exclusively "static" cross-sectional or equilibrium approach to a growing interest in transformations in social systems through time. Again, economists appear to have taken the lead, but other disciplines have also shown renewed interest in historical processes and in conceptions of systems that considered tensions and inherent sources of change. The developments in sociology have been particularly noteworthy, as an increasing number of scholars in that discipline began around mid-century to display disenchantment with the restrictive conventions that had bound most of the work of the inter-war years. The assumptions of extreme positivism made human conduct essentially purposeless and even mindless. The comparative perspective introduced into the general textbooks commonly stopped at a point of radical relativism: we do it this way, they do it that way. The closely associated emphasis on functionalism played up the close and self-equilibrating interdependence of elements in these unique social and cultural systems, to the neglect of discord, evolutionary drift, or purposive problem-solving. As these conceptions of social reality came to be recognized as inadequate for many purposes, the restive sociologists began to rediscover the older concerns of their field: theories of history, including Marxist conceptions of the changeful implications of conflict, and theories of social evolution, even though earlier formulations were recognized as naive. For the new and more complex conceptions of social systems, for the renewed quest for cross-sectional generalization, and especially for the revived interest in change, a major empirical facet of the modern world offered ample materials for study—the rapid transformation of societies under the impact of induced economic change.

In the United States, by 1949, there was a sufficient accumulation of scholarly interest in economic development to warrant the establishment of the Committee on Economic Growth of the Social Science Research Council, with an interdisciplinary membership. Although this book is in no sense sponsored by the Committee on Economic Growth, it could not have been written without my experience as a participant in its activities. The dedication of the book to the chairman of that Committee, Professor Simon Kuznets, symbolizes a collective debt as well as my high regard for an outstanding scholar. The conferences and other projects sponsored by the Committee have been concerned both with the continuing dynamics of industrialized societies and with the processes of change in areas just beginning modernization. The comparison of historical and contemporary industrialization is, indeed, a recurrent theme in the study of economic development—although scholarly specialization occasionally gives the impression that the subjects are quite unrelated.

This book may be regarded as an introduction to the series of studies on "Modernization of Traditional Societies." It is not a summary of the series, for the practical reason that it was completed before most of the others, and for the more important reason that I could not hope to command the range of information and analytical skills represented in the series as a whole. What I have attempted to do is to paint with a rather broad brush, in order to present an overview of the interplay of processes of change. Other volumes in the series will examine dynamic processes in closer perspective and finer detail, and thus not only "fill in the picture" but also correct the distortions that the grand view is likely to entail.

The writing was less easy than might be expected of a prolific (I shall not say prolix) producer of the written word, a fair proportion of my publications being on the subject at hand. A major motivational difficulty was one of ambivalence: the feeling, on the one hand, that the very extensive research and conscientious theorizing on "social aspects of economic development" should be, at long last, made available for students and other adult readers whose lives are bound to be affected by the unprecedented problems that the future will pose; the conviction, on the other hand, that little new was to be said beyond the admittedly scattered and occasionally obscure technical writings on the subject.

I have resolved part of the expositional problem, I trust happily, by extensive use of previous technical publications of mine. By permission of the respective editors and publishers I have adapted portions of several previously published papers, which are also identified by appropriate notes as they appear:

"Industrialization and Social Change," in Bert F. Hoselitz and Wilbert E. Moore, eds., *Industrialization and Society* (Paris and The Hague: UNESCO and Mouton, 1963), Chapter 15.

"The Social Framework of Economic Development," in Ralph Braibanti and Joseph J. Spengler, eds., *Traditions, Values, and Socio-Economic Development* (Durham, N.C.: Duke University Press, 1961), Chapter 2.

"Social Aspects of Economic Development," in Robert E. L. Faris, *Handbook of Modern Sociology* (Chicago: Rand McNally & Co., 1964), Chapter 23.

"Predicting Discontinuities in Social Change," *American Sociological Review*, 29: 331-38, June 1964.

I wish to record here my gratitude for the permissions granted.

My being a joint editor of the series of which this book is a part fortunately has not exempted me from the tender editorial mercies of Neil J. Smelser. For his many suggestions, both great and small, I am indeed thankful.

The contents of this book represent such distillation of past thought and research as I have been able to tolerate and such creative synthesis as I have been able to muster. It may not be my last word on the subject, but it is likely to be for a while. In a sense, this book was started more years ago than I should like to recall. It was completed during an initial period of scholarly freedom with the Russell Sage Foundation. This is my first, but I trust not my last, opportunity to thank the trustees and professional staff of the Foundation for their vote of confidence.

—WILBERT E. MOORE

*Princeton and New York*

# Contents

Commentaries on the contemporary world are noisy with violence. They tell us in tones somber or shrill that we are in the midst of, barely through, or imminently facing changes unprecedented in speed and size. The popular press and learned publications alike abound with the language of force and fury. There are "explosions" of information and population—the latter aided by a "baby boom" that is possibly and ambiguously sonic. There are "revolutions" of technology and aspirations, of communication and transportation, of relations between men and machines, along with political upheavals that at one time comprised the whole meaning of the term. The metaphor of revolution is adopted here with at least as much justification as elsewhere, though at the risk of indulging and perpetuating a kind of mindless cliché. Many of the revolutions and explosions that flow so easily from the tongues and pens of commentators are impressive in their speed and consequences, if not in their literal violence, but they are remarkably confined in locale. They exemplify an underlying fact about the modernized, industrialized, sophisticated segment of the world: change feeds on itself and escalates. *"Plus ça change, plus ça change"* is a truer and more perceptive aphorism than the original version, which heartened and deluded those eager to believe in stability. In human terms, the transformations that this book explores have excellent claims on our attention. The wonders of applied

CHAPTER ONE

# The World Industrial Revolution

science are real, and their influence is substantial in the bustling, economically advanced societies of the modern world. At present, however, social and attitudinal changes engage, titillate, or threaten more people than the paltry splendors of technology. Short of a nuclear war that would make human tenancy on earth unendurable, no quake that now shakes us is likely to be so extensive or profound as the universal quest for rapid economic growth. Old and massive civilizations, with their intricately detailed social usages, have proved but little more immune to the lures of modernization than have small and relatively unsophisticated tribal societies.

The quest for modernity and particularly for improved material wellbeing has appeared here and there and from time to time in the past. Some of these small flames sputtered and died, others lived and grew. The relatively recent successes have been spectacular, if disquieting to the beliefs and securities of older beneficiaries of economic growth: witness Japan and the Soviet Union as examples of rapid change and political truculence. But now—and *now* means mainly the period since World War II—"everybody wants to get into the act." Virtually no country or culture, no tribe or civilization, is immune to the sweeping ideological commitment to economic development in the broad sense if not industrialization in the precise sense.

It is ironic that the speed and extensity of social upheaval accompanying economic development (sometimes aiding, sometimes impeding) gives greater warrant to the term *revolution* than did the original models. The term *Industrial Revolution* was invented retrospectively to represent the transformation of the economic order that had taken place in England, western Europe, and the United States. Yet the development of an impersonal, monetary market for goods and of an almost impersonal market for labor long antedated the factory system.[1] The techniques of machine design and the use of nonhuman sources of power, the economies of scale and the consequent growth in fixed capital investments, the specialization of tasks and their intricate temporal coordination—all attributes of industrialism—evolved rather slowly and of course continue to change, but at an accelerating pace. Because of this accumulated experience, those areas that did not share in industrial evolution may now at least contemplate genuinely revolutionary change.

## REVOLUTIONARY PROSPECTS

Success is by no means uniformly assured in the current drive for economic development in areas previously out of the mainstream of rapid

[1] See Wilbert E. Moore, *Industrial Relations and the Social Order*, rev. ed. (New York: The Macmillan Company, 1951), pp. 17-24.

change. And even where substantial improvements in economic well-being do occur, Utopia will not have arrived. Problems multiply along with partial solutions. Nevertheless, the quest for economic modernization and continuing growth provides an element of world unity hitherto lacking. Pluralism of course persists, and is likely to continue to do so. Yet the rationalization of economic processes and organizations will provide a degree of instrumental unity to human endeavors, despite other differences of major magnitude.

Although doubt has been expressed, here and there, about the universality of higher economic aspirations, the proponents of cultural relativity, particularly in the form of differences in values that would provide an inhospitable environment for economic innovation, seem to have been mistaken. Several sorts of evidence point to the substantial nature of the change: the pronouncements and actions of political leaders, the political manifestations of "unrest," the "vote with the feet" represented by accelerated urbanization, the seemingly inexorable spread of the market system.

The magnitude of the ideological commitment to economic growth was not predicted by anthropologists and sociologists, who emphasized and exaggerated the integrity of traditional social systems and the diversity among them, or by economists, whose motivational assumptions were more nearly right but who understated the availability of entrepreneurs as agents of change and overstated the restrictions of resources and technology. In a sense, both groups of social scientists were trapped by their respective "classical models" and thereby missed precisely the transfers and demonstration effects that contemporary world history has exhibited. By giving seemingly proper attention to fine-grained analysis, by identifying and accounting for differences, social scientists generally missed the larger rush of events.

There are some morals to be drawn from this bit of intellectual history, but they need not detain us here. The matter of the moment, rather, is whether social scientists have learned a sufficient lesson so that some confidence can be placed in their views of the future. A clear and resounding affirmative would surely be an undue vote of confidence, but there are some reasons to suppose that substantially accurate if incomplete predictions are possible. At the very least, we can expect continuous ferment and dissatisfaction with current hardship, and though this discontent may not insure success, and could in fact impede it, there is no reason to expect a return to resignation.

The emerging unity of the world is anomalous in many ways. It is not political or ideological or cultural in any of the ordinary senses of these terms. It is a unity in discontent and revolutionary potential. By now we understand enough of the revolutionary process to know that some relief from ancient ills increases the demand for more. This is as true of the impoverished peasant or newly located urban slum-dweller in Africa or Asia or Latin America as it is of Negroes in the northern cities of the United States.

It may not be proper to hold industry in the strict sense accountable for these manifestations of discontent. But it is proper to attribute the shaking apart of traditional standards and social arrangements to the manifold facets of the industrial revolution, ranging from the widgets and gadgets spawned by the manufacturing process to the social dislocations and ideological alternatives associated with the quest for modernization.

## INDUSTRY AND INDUSTRIALISM

*Industry* refers to the fabrication of raw materials into intermediate components or finished products by primarily mechanical means dependent on inanimate sources of power. The prominence given to technology in this definition is not to be taken as some sort of technological determinism, or as denying the relevance of the factory system as a social organization. For analytical purposes, however, the social characteristics of industry are best viewed as conditions and consequences of its technical characteristics, and not as an intrinsic part of the definition. This distinction is further justified by the fact that the social organization of industry is only partly a correlate or derivative of technology. Similarly, of course, neither the products nor the technology of manufacture can be taken as reliably homogeneous, and some of the variability has crucial social significance: for example, as among labor-intensive production, mass production in the "modern classical" manner of large numbers of semiskilled workers closely paced by machines, or automated production monitored by a small number of skilled and responsible workers.

By the restricted definition of industry, discussion of a "world industrial revolution" may appear highly imaginative. Very little manufacturing is yet going on in the "underdeveloped areas"; its absence is a major reason for the designation. Yet we need extend the concept of industry or industrialization only slightly to see extensive efforts and effects. Agricultural mechanization, which does occur in some degree here and there in developing areas, clearly fits the restricted definition. The mechanization of transport yields services rather than goods, but the vehicles themselves are industrial products, and roads and airports are likely to require a considerable range of manufactured goods. Similarly, communications networks represent the products of industry somewhere, at home or abroad.

Industry then presents itself in the modern world by its products as well as its processes, and no country is likely to get far with its quest for economic growth without becoming a part of the industrial system at least in the utilization of products. Thus, improved seed varieties and chemical fertilizers for agriculture represent an aspect of industrialization, just as do antibiotics or insecticides for improved health.

This point needs emphasis, because it is likely to be missed if attention is given only to factories and their inhabitants. For example, it is certainly true that one may encounter urbanization without industrialization in the contemporary, as in the ancient, world. Yet in the modern era the burgeoning cities use mechanical surface transportation; pumps and perhaps purifying chemicals for water supplies; newspapers, telephones, and radios if not television for communication; hand saws and hammers if not engines and steel for construction, and so on.

As the products of industry spread to the developing areas, they become part of the impetus to change—not only and importantly in daily activities and styles of life but also in the demand for more and better products.

Several terms are often and properly used interchangeably, though their meaning differs in detail. We have been considering industry and industrialization and noting that the extensive use of manufactured products warrants a loosening of the term *industrialization* to include those products along with the factory system under mechanical power. Somewhat broader terms such as *economic growth* and *economic development* are also in common use. The advantage of the former term is that it can be precisely defined: increased real income per capita. Such a measure has a marked advantage in distinguishing bigger and better, for it is quite possible for a country to grow in the size of its economic product and in the number of inhabitants without the inhabitants being generally better off. Many "developing areas" are in fact faced with that treadmill-like prospect because of rapid population growth. But even if there is a genuine increase of real income per capita, the lot of the greater part of the population may be little better and possibly worse, as an economic elite enjoys the entire benefits of the growth attributed to the economy as a whole. That too can happen. Growth in this formal and numerical sense may have little effect on alleviating the lot of the ordinary inhabitant and little implication for future benefits. It cannot be dismissed lightly, however, for it is likely to increase revolutionary potential in the original, political sense.

The term *economic development* implies structural change in addition to mere increase in output. Development entails establishing or revamp-ing fiscal, financial, and fiduciary mechanisms. It involves institutional changes in the precise sense of alterations in the laws and other rules of conduct, organizational changes in the management of production and distribution, and, sooner or later, changes in the location, definition, and motivation of economic activity. Many of the changes implied by the term *economic development* are themselves not strictly economic: they are precedent to, accompaniments of, or early consequences of changes in the place of production, the shops, and the markets.

The most comprehensive term for the changes we are concerned with is *modernization,* a term deliberately selected for the series of studies of which this book is a part. Modernization may be political and social as well as economic. It means essentially becoming a member of the common pool of world knowledge and useful techniques, perhaps with-drawing much and adding little, but still sacrificing many time-encrusted customs for the sake of real or visionary benefits. Modernization involves adoption of the latest procedures in administrative organization and crime control, in mass communication and public health, in education and occupational placement, in city transportation and village organi-zation. Modernization means joining the modern world, and thus in-creasing its essential, though disorderly, unity.

The attention of this book will range over these characteristics of modernization, and others, but its central focus is symbolized by its title, *The Impact of Industry.* That focus has a number of justifications, and it is mete that they be made clear.

First, from a simply tactical standpoint, one must start somewhere in the attempt to observe, to understand, and to interpret the turmoil of contemporary events. It would be ridiculous to suppose that all these events can be linked to a mere change in mode of production or use of manufactured products. Yet the quest for economic improvement is ubiquitous, and its consequences are far-reaching. And it can be said with firmness that the industrial system provides the means if not the actual goals for desired changes that animate and aggravate the erst-while sleepy places so fascinating to tourists and purveyors of travelogs.

Second, there is a remarkably high degree of uniformity in the indus-trial system that transcends prior differences and current alternatives. Some of this uniformity is certainly imitative and therefore spurious in any sense of absolutes and invariable requirements. Such qualms occur properly to the social theorist, but the theorist or his inquisitive col-league also has some small responsibility to observed facts. The facts point to a notable consistency of modes of production and the attend-ant social organization, of modes of distribution and the attendant rules of conduct, and of modes of social placement and the attendant rationales in articulated values.

Third, the impact of industry may be anticipatory as well as consequential. There are preconditions for industrialization in addition to adaptive changes in sequential chains. The preconditions, once identified, constitute recipes for change, or at least the list of ingredients. This statement assumes of course a considerable measure of deliberate action rather than chance combinations, but that assumption is clearly valid for most of the contemporary world. This view of industrialization thus includes an ideological component, for economic development is doctrinal as well as merely instrumental, though the several components are both concretely and analytically distinguishable.

Fourth, industrialization appears to be a major and essential ingredient for substantial economic growth. The primarily agricultural character of most of the economic systems where developmental measures are now sought leads some scholars and technical advisors to seek developmental change solely within an agricultural context. It would be improper to deny the importance of improved agricultural technology and productivity, but we have already noted that such improvements are likely to include industrial products from somewhere. More importantly, there is no exception to the rule that substantial increases in per capita income have been accompanied by decreasing proportions of capital and labor devoted to agriculture. The supposed exceptions of Denmark and New Zealand as prosperous agricultural countries are belied by unmistakable facts. In both countries only a small minority of the labor force is engaged in agriculture.[2] This is not to say that fundamental change will come quickly to countries, such as China and India, that have massive agricultural populations, but it is to say that fabrication of food and fiber and eventually of other consumer goods and of machines is likely to be essential if substantial improvement in material well-being is to occur.

### DISCUSSION AGENDA

The central aim of this book is to explore the social significance of economic transformation or the industrial revolution. We thus seek to generalize from the older and newer experience already known and also to predict the probable course of change in areas just beginning the complex process of modernization. Part of the task is to assess as well as possible the uniform, the probable, and the highly variable

[2] The relation of occupational distributions to economic development is discussed in Chapter Four.

changes of the past and future. Chapter Two, "Convergence and Divergence," sets forth the theoretical and factual bases for that assessment. We shall there have occasion to note one more difficulty in the noisy metaphor of revolution, for although periods of tranquility may occur after some developmental measures, they merit the designation *economic stagnation;* successful industrialization is a continuous and not merely transitional change.

Though social systems are often viewed as web-like in their intricate interdependence, strands may be properly distinguished for observation and analysis, a point that has special relevance when the object is to study social transformations that may not be highly synchronized or even highly ordered. For such analysis some of the standard conceptual tools of the sociologist will prove useful. Chapter Three, "Conditions for Industrialization," considers resources, organization, institutions (standardized rules of conduct), and values. And since we are concerned with systems that are not completely integrated and especially with systems in transition, it is unsafe to infer attitudes and motivation from articulated values and standardized conduct; attitudes, too, must be viewed as sources of change or impediments to it.

To the degree that industrialization is at all determinate in its social consequences, the uniformities or limited ranges of alternatives should display themselves in at least two ways: as changes in social structure properly speaking, that is, in the way social life is ordered and organized, and as common *processes* of change that may cut across organizational boundaries. Chapter Four, "First-Order Consequences," sets forth those changes that are most closely linked to industrialization, both structurally and temporally. Chapter Five, "Reverberations," traces the consequences at some remove, and, often, of greater variability.

Since industrialization is not a fixed destination but a prospectively continuous and probably accelerating course of change, it is fitting, albeit hazardous, to attempt to prophesy. Chapter Six, "The Future of Industrial Societies," essays that task, with mixed motives of optimism and alarm. Though institutionalized rationality is a prominent feature of industrial systems, it cannot be said with confidence that rationality is gaining over the forces of unreason newly unleashed by industrial revolutions and persistent in industrial societies. It is quite unlikely that the lid can now be put back on the box; there remains the alternative of catching and controlling the ills that have escaped.

At irregular but short intervals the American can expect to have his peace and security threatened by an outbreak of violence in some foreign place he has probably not known about before. The emergence of new and unsteady nations and the struggle of the great powers for friends and influence in far places further unbalance a world political system not notably stable anyway. These manifestations of world interdependence without world unity in any of the ordinary senses of common values or social integration serve as brusque reminders that the changes that have reached and sometimes overwhelmed formerly colonial or otherwise stagnating areas are not necessarily benign.

Not all this political turmoil can be properly traced to the quest for economic development, and certainly not to that source alone. Political independence has had an appeal in its own right, and the competition for influence, especially that between the communist countries and the West, has added distinctly military overtones to the melody of technical assistance. Yet the eagerness of the leaders of new nations or other post-revolutionary regimes to revamp the economy is also notable. And whatever the ulterior political motives of the competing great powers, when they openly offer or are piteously petitioned for capital and technical advice they present the recipients with competing doctrines of economic development. The existence of these competing doctrines has important consequences

CHAPTER TWO

# Convergence and Divergence

for social analysis as well as for the great world of affairs. Doctrinal differences imply a diversity of routes and possibly of exact destinations in the way a country modernizes.

The task of this chapter is to explore this and other awkward circumstances: awkward because they make more difficult the attempt to generalize and predict the course of industrialization. Starting with the reasons for expecting some increase in the structural similarities between social systems, then turning to the reasons for expecting persistent and novel differences,[1] the chapter will conclude with a forthright appraisal of the current state of knowledge, and especially the state of ignorance relating to the possible outcomes of industrialization and the order in which they may appear.

### CREATION OF A COMMON CULTURE

The conflicting ideologies of development fostered by major political blocs in the modern world do not exhaust the relevant differences of opinion. Scholars, too, espouse divergent views, though on presumably different grounds. Whereas the ideological differences are normative—that is, how change ought to be—the scholarly differences are factual —that is, how change has been or will be. It is always most dramatic to represent divergent views as diametrically opposed. Usually, however, there are intermediate positions, and at times even the notion of a scale oversimplifies the disagreement.

One position emphasizes the similarity of industrial societies, and asserts or implies that newly developing areas will move toward a common social model as they industrialize. The supporting arguments are both empirical and theoretical. Inkeles and Bauer,[2] for example, summarize a variety of ways in which the Soviet Union resembles the "capitalist" industrial countries, despite differences in political systems. From their own and related studies they note similarities in access to education and the use of education as an occupational sorting mechanism; the relative evaluation of occupational categories; and intergenerational mobility rates. Where they can construct temporal trends, it appears that convergence is increasing, that is, that the Soviet Union has been "developing toward" a kind of standard model of advanced

[1] The principal theoretical bases for the discussion of similarities and differences in industrial societies are developed in Arnold S. Feldman and Wilbert E. Moore, "Industrialization and Industrialism: Convergence and Differentiation," *Transactions of the Fifth World Congress of Sociology*, 1962, Vol. **2**, pp. 151-69.

[2] Alex Inkeles and Raymond A. Bauer, *The Soviet Citizen* (Cambridge: Harvard University Press, 1959).

societies. Rose [3] adds some other common features, over a fairly wide range of economic advancement, and particularly highlights the uniform appearance of the small-family system as economies become industrialized. With respect to developing areas, Moore stated his position, since modified, as the "creation of a common culture." [4] Kerr, similarly, has argued for the predictability of the future of industrializing countries on the basis of the common characteristics of advanced countries:

> This particular history gets written mainly from the future into the present—what is currently happening comes from what is to be. The future is the cause and the present is the effect. [5]

Feldman and Moore used the typological characteristics of industrial societies as constituting the organizational and normative requirements for "commitment": performance of appropriate actions and the acceptance of the appropriate rules of conduct. [6] They too have since questioned the rigidity or invariability of the model they then employed; [7] they were criticized at the time by Singer, [8] who argued for the diversity of social evolution, and by Herskovits, [9] who argued that the hope for generalization across patently diverse cultures in transition was to be found in processes of change rather than in precise forms of social organization.

The underlying theory that leads to the expectation of growing similarity of industrial societies and of newly developing areas as they join the club might be phrased as "the theory of structural constraints." The essential idea is that a commercial-industrial system imposes certain organizational and institutional requirements not only on the economy

[3] Arnold Rose, ed., *The Institutions of Advanced Societies* (Minneapolis: University of Minnesota Press, 1958).

[4] Wilbert E. Moore, "Creation of a Common Culture," *Confluence*, 4 (July 1955), 229-38.

[5] Clark Kerr, "Changing Social Structures," in Wilbert E. Moore and Arnold S. Feldman, eds., *Labor Commitment and Social Change in Developing Areas* (New York: Social Science Research Council, 1960), Chap. 19; passage quoted from p. 358. See also Clark Kerr *et al.*, *Industrialism and Industrial Man* (Cambridge: Harvard University Press, 1960), esp. Part III, "The Road Ahead."

[6] Arnold S. Feldman and Wilbert E. Moore, "Spheres of Commitment," and "Postscript," in Moore and Feldman, eds., *Labor Commitment . . .* , Parts I and V.

[7] Feldman and Moore, "Industrialization and Industrialism . . . ," *op. cit.* See also Arnold S. Feldman, "The Nature of Industrial Societies," *World Politics*, 12 (July 1960), 614-20.

[8] Milton Singer, "Changing Craft Traditions in India," in Moore and Feldman, eds., *Labor Commitment . . .* , Chap. 14.

[9] Melville J. Herskovits, "The Organization of Work," in Moore and Feldman, eds., *Labor Commitment . . .* , Chap. 8, especially pp. 123-25.

but also on many other aspects of society. That idea in turn rests on a conception of close functional interdependence of the components of "social systems."

An opposite view has been expressed by Blumer:

I think that the evidence points clearly to the conclusion that industrialization, by its very make-up, can have no definite social effect. It is neutral and indifferent to what follows socially in its wake. To attribute specific social effects to it is to misread its character; to seek in it the causes of specific social happenings is to embark on a false journey.[10]

The specific context of Blumer's extreme conclusion is a discussion as to whether labor protest is a necessary consequence of early industrialization. To the question "Why is there such a high frequency of labor discontent and protest under early industrialization?" Blumer thinks the answer is that "early industrialization coincides frequently with situations of intense social change." Among such "coincident" changes he identifies urbanization, and modernization, "introducing new ideas of how to live and new conceptions of right and privileges." [11] Blumer asserts the independence from industrialization of these changes and others that he identifies (new interest groups, nationalistic movements). The independence is by no means self-evident. On the contrary.

Smelser, too, after recapitulating the sources of variability in the process of development, concludes: "It is virtually impossible to discover hard and fast empirical generalizations concerning the evolution of social structures during economic and social development." [12] He takes a position not unlike that of Herskovits, in that he identifies common processes of structural change associated with development: structural differentiation, integration, and social disturbances.

These somewhat reasonable differences of view among presumably reasonable students of economic development are disquieting. At the very least they require closer examination before one could properly cast a ballot for one position or another. Part, but only part, of the problem may be expressed as differing levels of generalization. Those who emphasize the commonalities of industrial societies will, for example, note the uniform use of administrative authority as a major way of coordinating highly specialized productive tasks. Thus the situation of the Russian factory manager is said to be very similar to that of his Amer-

[10] Herbert Blumer, "Early Industrialization and the Laboring Class," *Sociological Quarterly*, 1 (January 1960), 5-14; passage quoted from p. 9.

[11] *Ibid.*, p. 13.

[12] Neil J. Smelser, *The Sociology of Economic Life* (Englewood Cliffs, N.J.: Prentice-Hall, Inc., 1963), p. 106.

ican counterpart. Others, dissatisfied with such generalization, dwell on details, not all of which can be readily dismissed as trivial. The ultimate political accountability of Soviet and American factory managers differs, as does the conduct of relations with labor unions having highly unequal legal positions.

Another part of the problem of interpreting discordant interpretations derives from unequal and often unstated scholarly attitudes toward probabilities. The dedicated generalizer will identify a certain structural feature of industrial societies as "typical" and perhaps mistakenly imply that it is invariant, whereas his "relativistic" critic will point to contrary cases, and perhaps mistakenly imply that they are common rather than exceptional. A closely parallel difference of view distinguishes the theorist, who seeks out the uniformities in time and space, and the technical adviser, who must take account of variable particulars in the operating situation, down to the level of personality characteristics of public bureaucrats or private managers.[13] Each position tends to lead its tenants to impatience with the other.

Yet another source of difficulty derives from differing models of the social order and, inferentially, differing conceptions of the future. The proponents of convergence generally subscribe to a high degree of structural interdependence and functional integration in societies, as noted. Thus the system is viewed as highly determinate, *given* a major structural component. Internal disharmonies and external variation are then viewed as anachronistic, as inconsistencies that will disappear "eventually" or "in due course." The proponents of divergence emphasize pre-industrial differences among societies, differing rates and routes of change, and, often, they hold a less deterministic view of the social order at a given time and a more dynamic view of short-run flux and long-run evolution. In short, they doubt that "eventual stability" will ever arrive.

It must be said plainly that, at this level of discourse, the weight of evidence favors the dissidents, that is, those who doubt convergence now or ever. It was probably inevitable, however, that a middle course or position of compromise could be found. That middle course rests upon the following postulates or propositions, which will form the basis for most of the remainder of this book:

An industrialized or otherwise rationalized mode of economic production does indeed have both preconditions and consequences.

---

[13] See Wilbert E. Moore, "Developing Areas," in Paul F. Lazarsfeld, William H. Sewell, and Harold L. Wilensky, eds., *The Uses of Sociology* (New York: Basic Books, forthcoming, 1966). The basic line of reasoning derives from Feldman and Moore, "Industrialization and Industrialism . . . ," *op. cit.* See also Smelser, *op. cit.*, pp. 105-15.

These implications of industrialization must often be stated in general or "categorical" terms rather than with exact descriptive precision. In fact, some perfectly proper ways of asking questions of historical data on change will locate regularities beneath seeming empirical confusion. Other questions will, equally properly, reveal differences that cannot be subsumed under more general rubrics of commonality.

The probability of structural uniformity or convergence need not be perfect to be important. (Exceptions can then be examined with profit: Are they to be explained by special historical or contemporary circumstances? How is their apparent inconsistency accommodated? Can they be properly viewed as anachronistic, so that their disappearance may be reasonably predicted? Or are they indeed testimony to the looseness of social systems and the capacity of those systems to survive internal strains and disharmonies?)

Finally, some convergence may not be determined by any intrinsic demands traceable to industrialization but is instead explainable by simple imitation of prior patterns in advanced countries. (Indeed, one might expect some confusion of shadow and substance, whereby mere symbols of progress are adopted with the expectation that they will magically produce the reality.)

### PERSISTENT PLURALISM

The search for uniformities in the impact of industry, though legitimate and even laudable, cannot be totally successful in view of the crude and stubborn facts of variability. It will be useful to recapitulate the prime sources of variation, and the implications of that variation for the theoretical conception of social systems.[14]

By far the most common sociological approach to the transformation of underdeveloped areas of the world has rested upon a kind of model of change that was rarely made explicit. By exclusive attention to societies "in transition" students of economic development implied a preceding, traditional stage and a succeeding, industrial or advanced stage. The premodern stage was taken to be essentially static, the social structure persisting through a balance of interdependent forces and actions. Even more unrealistically, the fully modernized society was also taken to be static, though this assumption had to remain implicit because of its patent falsity.

Now what is initially interesting and instructive about this approach

[14] Much of this section has been adapted from Wilbert E. Moore, "Social Aspects of Economic Development," in Robert E. L. Faris, ed., *Handbook of Modern Sociology* (Chicago: Rand McNally & Co., 1964), Chap. 23.

is not its crudity but its utility. By concentrating on the manifold sources of contemporary evidence, by formalizing the kinds of structural changes to be expected from changes in so essential a societal feature as its system of production, scholars have compiled an impressive list of predictive principles, along with a partial accounting for variations.

The virtues and failures of each part of this conceptual model merit scrutiny. The conception of societies prior to modernization has not been so naive as to assume that they were or are alike. Sociologists have been in sufficiently close touch with anthropologists, if not with historians, to be aware of cultural diversity. Indeed, general textbooks commonly emphasize the range of social patterns and leave to the chapter headings the inferential fact that these are variations on themes rather than a random assembly of odd social practices. No, the mischief has arisen not primarily from the assumption of uniformity among traditional societies, but from the static connotations of the very term *traditional*. Traditional they may be in the sense of commonly justifying present practices in terms of precedent, and even in the extended sense that change in the past has not been rapid, continuous, and pervasive. Yet change is an intrinsic characteristic of all societies,[15] and the historic paths to the present inevitably and significantly affect the continuing paths to the future.

The lack of historical perspective has proved embarrassing. At the extreme this conceptual model has led to the *sociologistic error,* the assumption that history began yesterday, if not early this morning. This kind of temporal myopia has neglected not only the intrinsic sources and courses of change in all societies but also the important circumstance that most of the world has been under some form and degree of "Western" influence for periods of years and in some instances (such as, say, Latin America) for over four centuries. The results of this prolonged contact have been a great intermixture of cultural forms and social organizations. This intermixture of civilizations in turn has built new barriers to modernization or raised old ones while obviously starting the slow process of modernizations in some other sectors of social life. The imposition of a radical racial or ethnic distinction between managers and the managed, for example, has in many places added an irrational barrier to labor mobility on top of the real impediment of simple lack of trained skills. On the other hand, the commercialization of subsistence economies has clearly started them "on the way" to full participation in modern forms of production and distribution.

The identification of consequences and of impossible inconsistencies

---

[15] See Wilbert E. Moore, *Social Change* (Englewood Cliffs, N.J.: Prentice-Hall, Inc., 1963).

in the social order environing a modernized economy has been greatly aided, again paradoxically, by the unrealistic assumption that industrial societies are both static and homogeneous among themselves. This assumption has had sufficient proximity to fact in certain major respects to permit the use of the generalized features of industrial societies as a predictive destination for those now in the process of modernization.

Yet the future is still being created and at an accelerating pace of change in industrial societies. As they change, their resemblance to each other increases in some respects and scarcely at all in others. To match the unrealistic timelessness of the sociologistic error there is a kind of determinism of social structures that may be called the *functional equilibrium error*. The useful and indeed essential conception of social action as taking place in interdependent systems can be carried to the improper extreme of assuming not only that nothing changes from intrinsic sources, but also that any feature of the system is a key to all others. Societies are far looser aggregates than any biological organism, and at least the more complex animal species permit considerable ranges of structural variation and of individual differences. What the future imposes on the present for the developing areas is a resemblance but not a replication.

The assumption of uniformity among premodern societies must overlook manifold differences or treat them as essentially inconsequential. It must also incur the dangers of the sociologistic error by neglecting all sorts of cross-currents in the history of colonial and other societies that have experienced various external influences for various periods of time. The argument tends to go, however, that these variations, even if otherwise significant, wash out under the homogenizing influence of a compact and uniform set of requirements imposed by economic modernization. Feldman and Moore [16] argued against this view, maintaining that the way barriers to modernization are overcome not only affects the course of social change for a transitional period but also leaves a lasting residue in the social structure as a consequence of the measures taken for dealing with the problem. If, for example, underutilized land in large estates such as the Latin American *haciendas* gives rise to political discontent as well as low levels of agricultural production, the development measures will sooner or later include a land reform, and the kind of land reform will have enduring consequences for income distribution, capital formation, and labor recruitment.[17] Though such examples might be regarded as a tedious attention to detail, their significance is somewhat deeper, for they bear on a major theoretical (and practical)

[16] Feldman and Moore, "Industrialization and Industrialism . . . ," *op. cit.*
[17] See Wilbert E. Moore, *Industrialization and Labor* (Ithaca, N.Y.: Cornell University Press, 1951), Chap. 9.

question in the contemporary world: namely, the degree to which "advanced" societies are becoming alike. The legacy of history is one major reason for introducing a cautionary note in the recitals of the manifold ways in which industrialized societies resemble one another.

Variable conditions such as the size of countries, their natural resources, and their political and economic relations with other societies will affect not only the ease and speed with which they may be able to modernize, but also the type and scale of the industrial development that may take place.

Perhaps the major variable affecting the route or trajectory of change is the era or stage at which a political unit enters on a course of rapid economic change. Latecomers have available several models of historical transformation and of forms of political regime. They are bound neither by the rate nor by the sequence established by their predecessors in adding products and processes, forms of social organization, strategies of communication, or scientific knowledge. The new (or newly modernizing) nation might be compared with the shopper in an extensive and well-stocked supermarket. The shopper can select products from the shelves with virtually no regard to the date or order at which the goods entered the market's inventory.

The metaphor is exaggerated, of course, because a random or whimsical selection of the components available will violate all sorts of principles of interdependence and the functional relation of elements in social systems. Nevertheless, atomic power may be introduced before coal, radios before telephones, antibiotics before aspirin, and airfields before highways. And the supermarket analogy can be translated into somewhat more austere and significant terms. For some purposes it is useful to regard the entire world as a single social system, marked by extensive internal disharmonies but marked also by extensive transit of ideologies, knowledge, and products across conventional political boundaries.

A society persists not only through orderly continuity of established patterns but also through tension-management and change. This conception of society has certain advantages in terms of the "fit" of the model to observed characteristics, even those of a persistent or recurrent quality, such as social deviation. It has overwhelming advantages in dealing with the phenomena of leads and lags in situations of rapid transformation. An outstanding way in which both industrializing and industrial societies differ in social structure is in the allocation of power and the political structure of the state. If societies differ in their characteristic tensions, because of varying historic legacies and the ways these intersect with current problems of achieving social goals, then it is readily understandable that the principal agency functionally responsible for tension-management for the system as a whole, the state, will differ in its structure and forms of action.

The tension-management model also permits explicit recognition of one grossly evident fact difficult to reconcile with a kind of self-balancing mechanical system. That fact is the widespread use of deliberate change both in the attempted solution of identified problems and in the attempted achievement of goals associated with, say, economic development. A principal kind of tension, in other words, is the failure to achieve social ideals, whether those ideals be simply those of reliable conformity with norms or the approximation to new standards and aspirations.

If societies, whether industrializing or industrialized, differ one from the other in their characteristic tensions, it is not surprising that one outstanding structural correlate of those differences is to be found in the *political* structure of the state. Though the formal administrative structure of one ministry may look much like another, the kinds of controls imposed by the state and the ways the state maintains its own authority do differ substantially. This is true even among the "stable democracies," and the differences are greater as one encounters socialist and communist regimes.

Nor can these differences, at least, be derogated by reference to "mere details," or "lower levels of generalization." The problem of order is universal and thus highly general, and the variability in its partial solutions must be taken seriously as impairing the notion of social convergence through industrialization.

The world may be viewed as a single system for some purposes, particularly in view of the common pool of knowledge, ideas, and techniques. But that system retains strong elements of persistent pluralism. As developing areas accommodate their diverse cultures and histories, importing and inventing novel techniques and patterns in somewhat novel combinations, the disappearance of some of their archaic customs will not imply a total homogeneity of social life everywhere. Some of the new customs may be as exotic as the old despite their novelty.

In brief summary of the reasons for expecting some persistent diver-- gence among industrial and industrializing societies:

Preindustrial structural and cultural differences may persist because the economic system is not wholly determinate of other components of social systems, or they may leave residues because of the way they have been "eliminated."

The route or trajectory of change will differ according to historical period, alternative models and their eclectic combination, conditions such as size and natural resources, and relations with other societies.

These sources of variation argue for differences in the "weight" of various components of social systems, both temporally and as between countries, and in the role of the polity in tension-management (or in falling under revolutionary pressures).

Novelty, including accident as well as deliberately created change, may still occur; whether it will be then widely imitated cannot be fully predicted.

## DOUBTS AND UNCERTAINTIES [18]

Weaving a path through the controversial conclusions concerning the homogeneity of industrial societies would have been easier for sociologists if our basic knowledge of conditions and processes had been more complete. As we sought predictive answers to the multitude of questions posed by rapid social transformation in "underdeveloped areas," or were asked to provide answers for the use of agencies concerned with advisory policies, we naturally turned first to the kinds of intellectual equipment commonly used in our other studies. This equipment proved to be unsatisfactory in several respects, though often serving to develop and to order principles and generalizations that were both sound and, occasionally, useful. In particular, we found that "stable integration" models of society, interrupted only in a transitional stage, overstated both the similarity and the stability of all societies everywhere.

The manner in which history prevents its own replication creates difficulties in generalizations that will unite historical and contemporary experience and deal with the diversity that optional paths of change introduce. The situation is by no means desperate, as subsequent discussion of highly general patterns will demonstrate. It is, however, sufficiently serious not to be brushed aside lightly.

In addition to minimum, required sequences and results, what is needed, and is mostly not at hand, is the construction of limited-alternative or typological sequences where total generalization is improper. The first part of the desiderata can be partially fulfilled by the distinction between social preconditions of economic modernization and the concomitants and consequences of modernization. A summary of the reliable propositions relating to these components of social organization and its changes comprises the following chapters of this book. Even here the state of knowledge is far from satisfactory, for it provides little information on processes and rates of change and virtually nothing on the interplay among variables as they change. The "before-and-after" comparison is no mean achievement but it does not provide a clear map or timetable for the journey from one to the other.

It is unnecessary to repeat the explanation for the inhibitions imposed

[18] Several paragraphs of this section have been adapted from Moore, "Social Aspects of Economic Development," *op. cit.*

by a static model of social systems. What is more to the point is the way the problems posed by the attempt to order the phenomena of contemporary change that are refractory in their diversity has led to a recognition of kinds of ignorance that were previously ignored. An example is in order. It is generally assumed that a rising level of adult literacy and an increase in the average number of years of school completed and in the proportion of secondary school and college graduates in the population are somehow associated with economic development. The functional needs for literacy and for specialized training can be persuasively argued. Yet the historic course of changes in literacy and education levels in the older industrial societies is virtually unknown. Is education to be viewed primarily as a capital investment, a prerequisite for other changes, or as a consumption good that a prosperous economy can provide? The answer clearly has practical implications for the plans of developing countries [19] as well as theoretical interest for the sequences and rates of social transformation. A "before-and-after" model will not answer that kind of question; actual information on the timing of trends is required. The question was not likely to be asked except as a result of the interplay between policy questions and the evolution of conceptual models used by scholars.

The uncertainty concerning trends in education as they relate to other changes illustrates both the difficulty in assuming the primacy of "economic" change and the relative paucity of propositions that will simultaneously indicate the order and processes of social change.

When generalization fails, the dedicated generalizer is unlikely to conclude that the residue is simply chaotic. Rather, he is likely to attempt to identify a limited number of crucial variables and to construct typologies for different values of those variables. The typologies may be either cross-sectional—in which case the variables are likely to be treated as conditions—or sequential—in which case the variables are likely to be treated as relative rates of change. Actually few such typologies have been constructed.[20] The steadily expanding number of countries now embarking on deliberate developmental programs affords an unparalleled opportunity for studying structural change as it occurs, and it invites renewed attention to historical comparison for further testing of the limits of both convergence and divergence.

[19] See C. Arnold Anderson, "The Impact of the Educational System on Technological Change and Modernization," in Bert F. Hoselitz and Wilbert E. Moore, eds., *Industrialization and Society* (Paris and The Hague: UNESCO and Mouton, 1963), pp. 259-78.

[20] See, for example, Bert F. Hoselitz, "Patterns of Economic Growth," *Canadian Journal of Economics and Political Science*, **21** (November 1955), 416-31. Hoselitz further expanded and applied his typology in "Economic Policy and Economic Development," in Hugh G. J. Aitken, ed., *The State and Economic Growth* (New York: Social Science Research Council, 1959), Chap. 12.

The clamor for change is so general in the modern world that it hardly appears credible that most of the world's societies and cultures seemed sleepy and content through the opening four decades of the twentieth century. The contentment, we now have reason to believe, was either a sham or simple apathy in the face of apparently fixed iniquities. And the sleepiness was partly an apathetic sham and partly a distorted perception in the eye of the beholder. Yet it is certainly true that for most of the nonindustrial parts of the world—and in numerical terms, that means most of the world—the safest basis for predicting social behavior by the day or by the week or by the year was knowledge about "how it had always been." The winds of change have provoked a reconsideration of the seemingly somnolent societies, and the alacrity with which novelties have been embraced—in frequently bizarre combinations—has provoked scholarly soul-searching over the supposed inviolability of sanctified tradition. Theoretical structures shook, and first-hand observations were degraded into snapshot versions of a richer and more dynamic reality.

Though the discomfiture of the intellectuals provides a mean and temporary solace to prideful fools, the reshaping of science concerns us rather less than the reshaping of social systems. Yet the latter can be viewed only as chaotic or worthy of only journalistic reporting unless we

CHAPTER THREE

# Conditions for Industrialization

develop new instruments for systematic observation and for ordering observation into meaningful and predictive generalizations.

Among all the manifestations of discontent and disorder, of changes occasionally orderly and often volatile, the ones that engage our primary attention here are those that are somehow related to economic modernization. This may seem rather lacking in daring, and even lacking in a suitable sense for what is important, since many of the events that exemplify the end of quiet continuity present themselves in a political context. Disorder is intrinsically political, but the discontent that underlies it may have little to do with politics. We have urged the view that economic change is both a goal widely shared in underdeveloped areas and an instrument for the achievement of other goals such as education and health and even national power.

What, then, are the requirements for economic modernization or industrialization? They include the positive side of discontent, the quest for improvement. But they also include, ironically, a considerable measure of political order, a condition notably lacking in some of the very areas where the demand for economic improvement is articulate to the point of stridency.

Generalization is both important and hazardous.[1] At a minimum, a discussion of the social conditions for economic development should provide a systematic checklist for particular, local analyses. A somewhat more ambitious aim, which is the one sought here, is to establish types of relationship that will be applicable to any particular area by a process of filling in details. The maximum aim of theory is to establish highly general "laws" of economic growth. The hope for this achievement is, it appears, premature, although suggestive attempts have been made and are by no means fruitless.

Our objective is to outline a way of analyzing the social framework of economic development and to note at least some generalizations about the way various conditions interrelate. Our procedure will be to start with organization—that is, with action systems necessary for a modernized economy. We shall then consider the institutional order—the web of laws and less formal rules within which economic organization must act. Finally, we shall consider ideological and motivational elements: ultimate values, collective goals and aspirations, and the drives and purposes that animate individuals in the pursuit of economic activities. We shall thus be using a kind of metaphor of concentric circles, comparable

---

[1] Much of the balance of this chapter has been adapted, with major changes in organization, from Wilbert E. Moore, "The Social Framework of Economic Development," in Ralph Braibanti and Joseph J. Spengler, eds., *Tradition, Values, and Socio-Economic Development* (Durham, N.C.: Duke University Press, 1961), Chap. 2.

to our procedure in subsequent chapters in delineating the consequences of economic transformation.

It must be noted that we are following this procedure for analytical clarity, but the result will not be an order of priorities in terms of either time or urgency. Such priorities must differ according to the circumstances of particular areas. Nor is our procedure a strictly logical one, since goals must be considered as precedent to the means for their attainment. But the order adopted reflects the view that the gross goals of economic transformation are not in serious question. Ideological and motivational conditions almost appear as subtleties, as variables doubtless affecting the pace of change and even some of its detailed order, but often in ways less direct than, say, financial organizations or property laws.

## ORGANIZATION

The organizational requirements of modern economic systems are in one sense true by definition. That is, if industrialization is equated with factory production, all that remains is to specify the social characteristics of the latter. However, it is also true that almost any economic development will require rationalization of organization and the creation of concrete systems of action designed for specific and limited functions. Although forms of rationally constituted productive organization are probably much more common in preindustrial societies than is commonly supposed,[2] they constitute a central and pervasive characteristic of economically advanced societies.

The typical form of industrial and commercial organization as a complex network of positions and duties we shall consider as a first-order consequence of industrialization and postpone discussion of it until the following chapter. Our concern here is to identify a kind of minimum checklist of organizational requirements for economic modernization, without closely examining their exact forms as social systems. Our question can be put simply: What must be done in an organized way if a traditional economy is to be transformed into a modern one? Note that the underdeveloped economies of the contemporary world are far from homogeneous in their political and economic structures. Some have been colonial areas until very recently and thus have at least a veneer of modernity in their legal systems. Many have had some involvement in international trade and thus have at least a veneer of modernity in their commercial arrangements.

[2] See Stanley H. Udy Jr., *Organization of Work: A Comparative Analysis of Production Among Nonindustrial Peoples* (New Haven: HRAF Press, 1959).

*Resource Utilization*

Resources have significance for human affairs as means for the achievement of human ends, or as limiting conditions on the possibilities and costs of economic production. The soils that man has learned to use for growing food and fiber or for pasturing livestock, the stones and minerals that man has learned to transform into useful and ornamental objects or into ingredients or machines for fabricating those objects, and the inanimate sources of power that man has learned to harness as a supplement to his energy or that of domesticated animals—these resources are distributed very unevenly over the earth's surface. Any particular piece of the earth's land and water areas that has been marked out as constituting a political unit may be rich or poor in resources, or rich in some and poor in others. Of course, the picture may change through time, with new discoveries as a result of explorations for metals or fossil fuels such as coal and oil, or new techniques such as those that transformed uranium from a metal mainly useful as a ceramic glaze to an awesome source of power. Plans for industrialization must proceed from known resources, however, subject to change as geographical and technical discoveries are made.

The known resources and known techniques for their use need not be exclusively domestic, however. Even the European pioneers in industrialization relied on trade in raw materials as well as in finished products. The United States and later the Soviet Union with their large and richly endowed land areas were more nearly self-sufficient in resources, though not in capital and technology. As their industrial processes and consumer tastes demanded more and more exotic materials, the physical technology of transportation and the social technology of international trade made their economic growth less dependent on their own material endowments.[3]

Though trade and the accumulated technical knowledge that permits choice and substitution of products and processes have reduced the importance of local resources for industrial development, it remains true that unused raw materials make the developmental process easier. Exports of minerals or fossil fuels permit capital imports, and extraction and related activities will normally attract foreign capital.[4] Nonetheless

[3] See Joseph J. Spengler, "Summary, Synthesis, and Interpretation," in Spengler, ed., *Natural Resources and Economic Growth* (Washington, D.C.: Resources for the Future, 1961), pp. 275-303.

[4] See John H. Adler, "Changes in the Role of Resources at Different Stages of Economic Development," in Spengler, ed., *Natural Resources . . .* , pp. 48-70. See also Richard Hartshorne, "Geography and Economic Growth," in Norton Ginsburg, ed., *Essays on Geography and Economic Development* (Chicago: Department of Geography, University of Chicago, 1960), Chap. 1.

the possibility and rate of economic growth may be less affected by resources than is the exact composition of production. That is, where particular resources are locally available, their fabrication is more likely to be a leading component of industrial output. This is one of the principal reasons that food processing and textile manufacturing figure prominently in early stages of industrialization, since the resources used are primarily agricultural in origin.

Very small countries that are also poor in natural resources will experience unusual difficulties in achieving substantial economic growth. Those that have succeeded—Switzerland, Denmark, Belgium, Netherlands, and, more recently, Hong Kong and Puerto Rico—have done so in part by importing raw materials and exporting finished products. Their success has rested, therefore, on increasing the effectiveness of use of their *human* resources. Small countries in Africa and Latin America may also be able to overcome the limits set by poor resources, but only if they become in a sense part of larger economic units through trade and simultaneously upgrade the qualities of their potential workers.

*Financial Organization*

Banks and other financial organizations are necessary as a means of assembling and distributing funds and credits. Unless the state is the exclusive investor, banks and similar organizations are needed to tap the savings that commonly exist even in poor countries. Since the assembling of the various "factors of production" is not an instantaneous process and often requires the making of plans and placing of orders months and even years in advance of the intended completion date, a system of debts and credits is essential.

It is banal to observe that the principal economic problem of the underdeveloped areas is the shortage of capital. However, some aspects of the problem are far from elementary. And there is ample theoretical and empirical reason to doubt that large capital supplies would automatically solve the remaining difficulties of economic development. The historical record in the countries now well advanced in industrialization indicates that a high rate of savings (or *capital formation*) does not necessarily produce a high rate of gross output or output per capita. As Kuznets concludes from his review of historical trends in capital formation,

Capital formation does not matter as much as capital utilization. And utilization depends upon a host of economic and social conditions which sometimes permit attainment of high rates of growth with little capital, but at other times impede the growth-inducing effect of even large amounts of capital.[5]

Substantial savings cannot be expected in tribal or other subsistence economies. Peasant and other agrarian economies, however, may have considerable "frozen" savings not put to productive use. The savings of a family may be almost entirely represented by gold and precious stones made up into jewelry for women (or, occasionally for men also). Gold and silver coins may be accumulated and hoarded. The assets embodied by jewelry may be used as security for loans (commonly at usurious rates) or even converted to cash by sale in cases of emergency. But these attempts at self-insurance provide little or no benefit to the economy or return to the hoarders. The shortage of developmental capital may thus derive partly from the lack of confidence in the safety of investment and in the stability of currencies, and from the lack of reliable channels of investment for the small investor. Existing investment channels, if available and utilized at all, may be overly conservative or may divert savings to relatively unproductive uses such as loans that help the farm family survive until the next crop is harvested but without improvements in capital or techniques that would increase productivity.

The harnessing of savings for capital expansion is both a condition and consequence of industrialization in something more than a definitional sense. Yet the rates and mechanisms of doing so cannot be generalized through time and space. The historic record is mixed, as just noted, and the contemporary developing areas add further types of variation.

Socialist states can attempt, more or less effectively, to capture and utilize all savings by collectivizing all forms of production and taking all profits either directly or through taxation. Other economies must find alternative ways to induce savers to become investors rather than hoarders. In free enterprise systems, business profits become a principal source of capital accumulation through being reinvested in the same or other activities. Profits, however, may simply be spent on increased current consumption by their recipients. In many underdeveloped countries, increased luxury consumption has negative effects on the economy, since it is likely to involve luxury imports. This provides no effective increased market for domestically produced goods, and uses up scarce foreign exchange needed for capital imports. Foreign investments pose a special problem, for the profits may be neither spent nor invested locally, but

[5] Simon Kuznets, *Quantitative Aspects of the Economic Growth of Nations: VI. Long-Term Trends in Capital Formation Proportions,* Supplement to *Economic Development and Cultural Change,* **9,** 4 (July 1961), 56.

instead be repatriated for the benefit of the investors, to spend or invest in the country supplying the original capital.

Even high profits may not be sufficient to divert savings from one economic sector to another: for example, from agriculture to industry. The risks may be judged as disproportionately higher. In addition, unfamiliar organization and technology are involved. These possibly rational considerations are often supported by nonrational ones. This is particularly true where ownership of land involves the principal basis of both security and prestige in the traditional social structure, while newer economic activities at best provide merely money but not aristocratic social standing.

Large-scale industrial production normally requires capital beyond the means of even wealthy families. There are three fundamental alternative ways of getting the necessary capital: from a large foreign corporation, from a domestic corporation that will pool the resources of many investors, or from the government, which uses its taxing or borrowing power to acquire the funds. There are, of course, many varieties and mixtures of the means of assembling savings and directing them toward investments consistent with continuous economic growth. The machinery of investment is a necessary counterpart of the organization of production.

In newly developing areas, the needs for investment to create expanded productive facilities intersect the rising demand for current consumption. Even if there were no population growth—and that is a seriously complicating factor, as we shall see—the poverty that is a major incentive for economic development is also a major deterrent to rapid growth. For the private investor in the oldest industrial economies, savings represent deferred consumption. In the meantime, he receives additional income, in the form of interest, dividends, or trading profits, from investing his savings. The desperately poor are unlikely to afford voluntarily the luxury of postponing consumption, unless this is somehow linked to the quest for economic security and familial obligations toward children.

Transportation and communications systems are also requisite conditions both for national economic integration and for links with the industrial and commercial world. With the rich pool of accumulated technology now available to newly developing areas, their forms of transportation and communication at any given time may not exactly duplicate those of advanced industrial countries, and certainly there is no need to replicate the original sequence of development. Air strips may be built before hard-surfaced roads, and radio stations before telephone lines. Still, the various forms of transportation and communication in current use in advanced countries have somewhat distinct functions, and newly developing countries are likely through time to broaden their range of facilities.

Resource utilization, commercial and financial organization, and a network of transportation and communication comprise the minimum essential organizational conditions for industrialization. A host of other organizational forms are highly correlated with economic modernization but scarcely qualify as prior conditions. Research institutes, public health services, or an electric-power grid may greatly facilitate economic growth, but there are enough examples of alternative arrangements to caution us against viewing them as necessities.

### THE INSTITUTIONAL ORDER

It is the general function of institutions, as complexes of norms or rules of conduct, to relate standard patterns of actions in a society—often encompassed in concrete social organizations—to the general system of functional requirements and values of that society. This statement, although cryptic, has some implications that are substantive as well as conceptual. The set of prescriptions and expectations comprised by the institution of monogamous marriage, for example, appears, correctly, to have primary relevance to family and household composition. By the same token, however, the institution has relevance for the heterosexual relations of adults generally, the socialization of the young, the mode of distribution of goods and services, the modes of assigning general social status, and—in more attenuated ways—maintenance of order and preservation of values. In other words, assignment of an institutional complex to a particular functional area—familial, economic, political, religious—is always in some measure improper. It is precisely one function of institutions that they be *relational*, that is, that they provide the bonds or cement among particular patterns of social action.

These general comments are prompted by the circumstance that we shall here be considering the significance of institutions that are in the first instance "economic," before moving to other institutional requirements. In no instance, however, is the designation precise, since we shall be dealing always with *degrees* of relevance for the production and distribution of goods and service.

*"Economic" Institutions*

Traditional economic analysis would have dealt with land, labor, and capital as "factors of production" and later theorists would add "entrepreneurship" or "organization." This conceptual famework has basic difficulties, as there is really little sensible or useful distinction between land and capital, and entrepreneurship may properly be considered a particular kind of skilled labor. It seems preferable, therefore, to adopt a somewhat different conceptual scheme. We shall here deal with three interrelated institutional complexes—property, labor, and exchange. All three seem to define aspects of relations between persons and "things"— their control, transformation, and distribution. However, all also define social relationship—between owners and nonowners, between persons performing complementary tasks, between sellers and buyers. No society is or could be lacking in rules governing such relationships, but their form and content differ and these differences are centrally relevant for the possibilities of economic development.

A *property* relationship is at the minimum triadic: the person or other social unit, the object or locus of scarce values, and the potential challenger to "rights." Property relationships may also be very complex, with various social units holding common or diversified rights in the same locus of value, varying rights of disposal, transfer, use and appropriation of increase.[6]

The important point in the present context is that the property systems of most underdeveloped areas do not favor modern forms of economic enterprise. This is generally true, for example, of the older property laws and practices in Latin America. The application in the Spanish colonies of quasi-feudal land-tenure conceptions (often through the specific forms of the *repartimiento* and *encomienda,* which "entrusted" indigenous populations and their labor to landlords) encouraged large estates but not necessarily their efficient operation or easy transfer to more efficient producers. The *hacienda* system and many other forms of plantation agriculture have often been wasteful of both labor and capital (land and its fertility). Perhaps most importantly it established the basis of a socioeconomic elite dedicated to traditional economic and social forms.

Modifications of traditional property systems have not necessarily brought them "closer" to the institutional requirements for economic development. Land reforms, for example, may lead to more intensive utilization but often still with archaic techniques and with overcapitalization of equipment that must be held by each cultivator of a small holding. The Mexican *Ejido,* which like most land reforms was undertaken primarily in the interests of social justice rather than economic modernization, has discouraged transferability of property and has prob-

---

[6] See Wilbert E. Moore, "The Emergence of New Property Conceptions in America," *Journal of Legal and Political Sociology,* 1, 3-4 (April 1943), 34-58.

ably contributed to hidden unemployment in agriculture.[7] Put in the bluntest possible terms, peasant proprietorship is more likely to impede than to facilitate economic development.

Any property system consistent with modern forms of production tends to "expropriate" the worker from ownership of most tools of production. The avoidance of this by socialist organization or nationalization of capital is only partial and partly fictitious, since essential controls of capital allocation and disposition remain in the hands of relatively limited numbers. The economies of scale characteristic of modern economic enterprise can be achieved only by correlative unity of control, however the ancillary rights and benefits may be distributed. Those same economies of scale are likely to require collective forms of proprietorship, whether through the state or through the private corporation that mobilizes the financial resources of many individual investors.

*Labor* provides a second major focus for economic institutions. The norms governing productive work are aspects of more general norms that control status and role assignments in a continuing social order. In a nonindustrial or, more properly, in a nonmarket economy the separation of useful activities into "labor" and "other" is likely to be difficult and abstract, except with reference to the production of physical goods.[8] Any society is characterized by considerable specialization of roles, including in this narrow sense, productive roles. Generally, although not entirely,[9] this specialization in nonindustrial societies is determined on grounds of age, sex, kinship, and hereditary social position. Competence is then developed for predetermined positions in the process of socializing the young. Such an institutional structure is likely to function adequately for limited specialization and minimal change. It is scarcely suitable for an economic system that entails extensive specialization and relatively rapid change in occupational structure. The difficulty of institutional adaptation is made more acute by the circumstances that new forms of demand for labor represent a radical shift in social role, and are intrusive in the traditional structure.

Among the many institutional difficulties with respect to labor mobility, several may be especially noted. Strong traditional attachments to the land (with ancillary handicraft production) discourage movement to other modes of production without the pressure of poverty.

---

[7] See Wilbert E. Moore, *Industrialization and Labor* (Ithaca, N.Y.: Cornell University Press, 1951), pp. 237-38.

[8] See Wilbert E. Moore, "The Exportability of the 'Labor Force' Concept," *American Sociological Review*, **18** (February 1953), 68-72.

[9] Udy, *op. cit.*

Moreover, where large-scale agriculture is the norm, various covert forms of peonage or debt servitude are by no means unknown.

The problem of securing enterprisers, managers, and technicians for modern economic production is partly educational—the sheer undersupply of skills. The institutional order in the normative sense is also relevant, however. Traditional forms of division of labor have placed considerable value on public administration and the older professions, less on business administration, risk-taking investments, or various kinds of engineering. It is not clear how acute this institutional barrier to development may be, but there is some suggestion [10] that both managerial innovation and capital formation are hindered by persistent high evaluation of a "leisure class" and the choice of current luxury consumption over reinvestment and productive expansion.

The third institutional complex of primary relevance to the economy is that of *exchange*. Some minimum form of exchange prevails in any society for transfer of products from the specialized producer to the general consumer. However, the elaboration of exchange relationships is likely to be limited by the degree of productive specialization. Typically, too, exchange relations are closely intertwined with other social bonds in preindustrial societies. Even "markets," which are a feature of many agrarian areas, may involve a complex of social relationships and of barter according to traditional terms of trade rather than consideration of current supply and demand. [11]

Economic development depends upon institutional transformation in the direction of "impersonal" markets, not only for goods but also for labor. These are linked by profits, salaries, and wages, all of which are virtually meaningless in the absence of a commodity market. Wherever transportation facilities and communications permit in Africa, Asia, and Latin America, there is evidence of the gradual or abrupt transformation of traditional trading relations into something approximating the economists' model of markets. [12]

If one were to attempt a one-word summary of the institutional requirements of economic development, that word would be *mobility*. Property rights, consumer goods, and laborers must be freed from traditional bonds and restraints, from aristocratic traditions, quasi-feudal

[10] See Frederick Harbison and Charles A. Myers, *Management in the Industrial World* (New York: McGraw-Hill Book Company, 1959).

[11] See Talcott Parsons and Neil Smelser, *Economy and Society* (New York: Free Press of Glencoe, Inc., 1956).

[12] See Richard H. Holton, "Changing Demand and Consumption," in Wilbert E. Moore and Arnold S. Feldman, eds., *Labor Commitment and Social Change in Developing Areas* (New York: Social Science Research Council, 1960), Chap. 11.

arrangements, paternalistic and other multibonded relations. Such mobility necessarily creates tensions and readjustments. The orderliness of social life becomes and remains precarious, for there is no stable future time unless the modernizing efforts themselves fail.

*Order and Change*

In addition to those normative complexes that have primary relevance for the production and distribution of goods, there are other systems of values and prescriptions for behavior that modify or affect the course of economic development. We need to note here especially the problems of maintaining a sufficient degree of reliability and persistent predictability in social action, on the one hand, while the system is embarked on programs of rapid change and encountering its side effects.

Because manufacturing, as distinct from many aspects of trade and commerce, depends heavily on fixed capital installations, *political order* is a prime requisite for industrialization. This requirement is accentuated by the extensive development of a credit structure, often on long-term bases, that characterizes both the capitalization and the trade of industrial societies. The geographical extent of political order is also of some importance, since the "factors of production" for manufacturing must typically be assembled from scattered places that often lie within different national boundaries.

The notable political instability in many underdeveloped countries cannot fail, accordingly, to have an adverse effect on many forms of economic development. Mere transfers of power, with or without electoral sanction, may have little consequence, of course, but rapid changes in legislation and administration set up difficult if not impossible conditions for long-term planning and commitment of resources.

Though order is essential, it serves as a framework for massive changes. At early stages of industrialization, which is our focus here, a structural revolution in productive processes is involved. But that revolution is not a single event or a mere transition from a stable condition of poverty to a stable condition of wealth. Change becomes a continuing and often accelerating state of the social system.

Change, in fact, becomes institutionalized. This is most obviously the situation with reference to the encouragement of *science and technology*. Initially it is the systematic knowledge of the nonhuman environment that is paramount, but large-scale production and distribution and the persistently troublesome questions of human aspirations also make *social* knowledge relevant. The development of exact science and its application to particular problems in the form of various technologies rest upon education systems and research establishments, but these in turn rest upon norms that specify a rational, problem-solving orientation to the natural and social universe.

It is often noted that latecomers in the process of economic development are heirs to the accumulated technology of the older industrial areas, and thus do not need a complete recapitulation of the sequence or the time initially required for that accumulation. It is less often noted that any technology is part of a functional context, beginning with such mundane considerations as parts' suppliers and repair facilities, extending to skilled technicians, and finally to the institutional system itself. When we add the important qualification that many technical developments are "labor-saving," which is not a matter of fundamental economic importance in most underdeveloped areas, we have seriously modified the easy acceptance of the "acceleration principle" in the diffusion of technology.

In most societies in the history of the world, change has been largely unintentional and often simply the response to natural or social crises. It is a special feature of industrial societies that a great deal of social, including economic, change is deliberate. This is closely related to the norms governing science and technology, particularly as the latter are viewed in an appropriately extended sense. Historically it appears that the development of change as a *norm* was slow and characteristic precisely of inventors and entrepreneurs. In the contemporary world the primary source of this institutional transformation is likely to be governmental, only gradually extending to more "private" sectors of social systems. The acceptance and active fostering of the "rational spirit" in all aspects of social behavior,[13] with its attendant subversion of the power of tradition, appears to be a necessary if often unwelcome correlate of economic growth.

### IDEOLOGY AND MOTIVES

Standard anthropological and sociological analyses of societies, cultures, and lesser social systems place great emphasis on the integrative function of *values*. The emphasis is not misplaced, if it stops with the functional importance of ultimate explanations and justifications for specific beliefs, rules, and patterns of action. The emphasis is misplaced, however, if such values are regarded as immutable, and therefore as

[13] See Wilbert E. Moore, "Measurement of Organizational and Institutional Implications of Changes in Productive Technology," in International Social Science Council, *Social, Economic and Technological Change: A Theoretical Approach* (Paris, 1958), pp. 229-59.

"permanent" sources of differences in social systems or at least as tremendous barriers to the acceptance of any such social novelty as new forms of economic activity. Precisely because of their pervasive, integrative function, values are likely to be slow to change, and to furnish resistance to innovation in subtle ways. Nevertheless, some value changes do occur, and "traditions" may evolve, become adapted to objective changes in social conditions, and even decline.[14] Crude historical experience also offers ample evidence that ideologies are transferable between social systems. Thus belief systems ranging from the strictly religious (such as Christianity or Islam) to the seemingly secular (such as economic development) have shown remarkable powers of expansion among otherwise diverse cultures.

One of the most commonly noted features of industrial societies is their internal diversification. A complex division of economic function is integrated through the impersonal operation of the market or the quasi-impersonal discipline of administrative organizations. Urbanization and other forms of geographical mobility potentially bring together people of highly diverse backgrounds. Income and status differences result in quite variable styles of life. A multitude of associations vie for members, whether to press economic and political interests or simply to represent expressive and recreational affinities.

Behind such diversity there are three principal common orientations: a minimal cognitive consensus, an acquiescence in if not positive acceptance of a normative order without which coordination could not emerge from specialization, and a minimal consensus on ultimate values.

The importance of formal education in providing common cognitive orientations will be noted in later discussion. Many less formal agencies of socialization operate also—at work, in the market, in urban neighborhoods. Increasingly, also, "mass communication" media are used both for quick dissemination of information and for propaganda and persuasion. The person in transitional situations must learn a multitude of facts and skills, from survival tactics in urban traffic to the arbitrary divisions of life's activities into temporal units.

The normative order, which had our attention in the preceding section of the chapter, needs one point of further emphasis here. It is in the general nature of rules to be specific and therefore to arise in particular action contexts: the family, the work place, the market, the school, the church. It does appear, however, that some more general "normative orientations"—generalized principles of correct conduct—may

---

[14] See Bert F. Hoselitz, "Tradition and Economic Growth," in Braibanti and Spengler, eds., *Tradition, Values, and Socio-Economic Development*, Chap. 3.

operate pervasively. Promptness and a rational orientation to decisions are two examples of such generalized norms in industrial systems. The transferability of such norms from one action pattern to another aids individual role-playing: "If in doubt, follow the general rule." Transferability also serves as an indirect, integrative linkage among highly specialized contexts of social behavior.

A minimum value consensus is also a theoretical necessity of a viable social order. Not only is the normative order usually referable to common values, but such values may be given specific ideological explication and thus serve as direct incentives to appropriate action.[15] Standards of equity and justice; the allocation of wealth, power, and position; the maintenance of institutional balance—these serve as value premises for particular sets of rules. Additionally, political and religious ideologies may provide goals as well as standards of conduct.

*Beliefs: Sacred and Profane*

The debate over the importance of Protestantism in the rise of capitalism is scarcely relevant to most developing areas, yet the problem of ultimate values is still critical. Collectivist ideologies, for example, may assume religious overtones, promising, among other things, that worldly immortality can be gained by developing the economy for generations yet unborn ("building the socialist fatherland"). Nationalism and patriotism always have religious elements, whether linked to traditional religious beliefs or not.

Subtle questions remain, however, concerning religious beliefs. As we noted briefly when discussing motivation and enterprise, the achievement orientations encouraged in some parts of Protestant Christianity may be either absent or less socially disciplined in other religious systems. Does the other-worldliness of Hinduism or Roman Catholicism, combined with an emphasis on acceptance and adaptation instead of active improvement, preclude economic development? Does the somewhat more hedonistic other-worldliness of Islam, coupled with an authoritarian view of worldly power, have similar negative effects? The questions multiply, but the answers do not.

The questions are, to repeat, subtle, since the gross evidence of a strongly secular goal-orientation toward economic growth is manifested "everywhere." Even in cultures traditionally based on an ideological system that emphasized other-worldliness, the desire for change in this

15 See Joseph J. Spengler, "Theory, Ideology, and Non-Economic Values, and Politico-Economic Development," in Braibanti and Spengler, eds., *Tradition, Values, and Socio-Economic Development,* Chap. 1.

world is constantly increasing. Indeed, the desire for such change has itself become a *spiritual* force of great importance in those areas of the world.[16]

When translated into motivational terms, the goal of economic growth is most widely and enthusiastically endorsed as producing an improvement in the material conditions of life. Yet there are other uses for wealth, including patronage of the arts, construction of monuments and monumental buildings, contributing to cultivated knowledge, and purchasing destructive weapons. It is the utility of economic growth as a kind of "universal means" that mainly accounts for its "ultimate" quality, an end in itself. To achieve that end changes in practices and institutions become the requisite means.

The ideological goal is a necessary but by no means sufficient condition for social transformation. The "means" turn out to be new patterns of daily existence, and thus in conflict with an intricately interrelated social structure. These patterns of behavior and their normative codes in turn relate to goals and values other than economic development or material well-being. Since material well-being is not the sole goal of any society, and could not be if it is to survive as a viable system, the value conflict is not trivial or simply based on temporary ignorance or misunderstanding.

The undoubted costs (in terms of value sacrifices) entailed in economic development may be partially offset not only by new distributive rewards of one sort or another, but by additional collective ideologies.

It is commonly, and probably correctly, assumed that wherever economic development becomes a matter of public policy (and that is nearly everywhere) the state is likely to play an active role, at least in surmounting barriers. Although the economic activity of the state in the historic "laissez-faire" economies should not be minimized, there is ample reason to assume that the contemporary state will figure more largely as an agent of growth than was true in the past.[17] Questions of political loyalty and participation therefore assume an importance directly relevant to economic development, in addition to the role of the state as the focus of national integration and identity and the ultimate enforcement agency for social codes.

The repeated association between deliberate economic development and extreme nationalism is surely not accidental. Nationalism presents

[16] See Arnold S. Feldman and Wilbert E. Moore, "Commitment of the Industrial Labor Force," in Moore and Feldman, eds., *Labor Commitment* . . . , Chap. 1.

[17] See Hugh G. J. Aitken, ed., *The State and Economic Growth* (New York: Social Science Research Council, 1959); Karl de Schweinitz Jr., *Industrialization and Democracy: Economic Necessities and Political Possibilities* (New York: Free Press of Glencoe, Inc., 1964).

an essentially nonrational unifying force that may ease and rationalize the hardships of personal change. As Smelser has observed,

Because the existing commitments and methods of integration are deeply rooted in the organization of traditional society, a very generalized and powerful commitment is required to pry individuals from these attachments.[18]

In his view, "xenophobic national aspirations" and political ideologies such as socialism are the functional equivalents of religious values such as Protestantism. In new nations the forms of nationalism include using the former colonial power as a scapegoat for present dissatisfactions and the attempt to establish an older history and continuity of traditions prior to the interregnum of the colonial period. And it is especially in the former colonies that a prior sense of national, or even cultural, identity scarcely existed. When the transition to independence is also accompanied by extensive efforts at economic revolution, various intermediate social structures that shared or captured loyalties in the pre-industrial system are undermined. Nationalism—often in the garb of Arab or Indian or African socialism—is offered as a source of identity to substitute for the tribe or village. Success in establishing a nationalist ideology provides a rationale for the multitude of changes in way of life, though we shall discuss later the low probability that genuinely democratic institutions will quickly emerge. Failure to achieve national political unity is likely to retard or prevent programs of economic change.

### Motives and Enterprise

Human motives are largely the product of socialization, that is, cognitive learning and the internalization of values and social codes. In a highly integrated and stable social order individual motives might be viewed simply as the counterparts of values and institutions attributable to the collectivity as such. The justifications for their separate consideration are several. (1) Even in the most "tightly structured" social system, values, institutions, and specific organizational commitments involve some cross-pressures and permit some latitude for choice and innovation. (2) The socialization process itself will scarcely produce precise duplication and maintenance of traditional behavior and may provide an important key to the direction of change in social systems. (3) Particularly in social systems where novel forms of behavior, such as new productive and distributive systems, are being introduced, the motiva-

[18] Neil J. Smelser, "Mechanisms of Change and Adjustment to Change," in Bert F. Hoselitz and Wilbert E. Moore, eds., *Industrialization and Society* (Paris and The Hague: UNESCO and Mouton, 1963), Chap. 2; passage quoted from pp. 38-39.

tional counterparts of the social transition require close examination leading to more highly refined conclusions than the motivational inferences that may be drawn from analysis of stable social structures. It is possible that "the content of men's minds" may be altered somewhat independently of changes in structures and institutions.[19]

One important theoretical implication of this way of posing the issues should be noted. Sociologists and psychologists have commonly dealt only with the socialization of children, and have too readily accepted Freudian dogma concerning the exclusive importance of early emotional experience. What we are dealing with is a large measure of *adult* socialization in the behavioral aspects of economic development. That is, prior to the establishment of "industrial traditions" and their presumable perpetuation from generation to generation, we are interested in precisely the departures from traditional norms and canons of behavior and the process whereby adults—even if typically young adults—become involved in and perhaps emotionally committed to novel social situations.

Implicit in the requirement of new work relations and forms of productive organization is the necessity of subjective attitudes and objective incentives favorable to new tasks and conditions of employment. More empirical research and theoretical work have probably been done on this aspect of industrialization than on any other. The results, however, yield more in identifying pressures, barriers, and incentives regarding labor recruitment than they do in more complex propositions where many forces operate concurrently and even discordantly.

Many devices have been used to get workers involved in new economic enterprises, and many of them have not been pretty.[20] Direct coercion, ranging from slavery to military conscription, has been far from rare. After slavery became unfashionable and illegal, colonial authorities in Africa hit upon a more refined use of political power: the power of taxation. Taxes were made payable only in money, which thus required participation in the developing labor market.[21] Even voluntary entrance of workers into the labor market and new ways of gaining a livelihood more often than not has been a choice between evils. Young men and women have left their native villages because of social conflict or

[19] See Spengler, *op. cit.*

[20] For an extensive summary of labor recruitment and utilization in newly developing areas, see Wilbert E. Moore, *Industrialization and Labor*. From subsequent evidence it appears that the resistances to change were taken too seriously in that book.

[21] See Wilbert E. Moore, "The Adaptation of African Labor Systems to Social Change," in Melville J. Herskovits and Mitchell Harwitz, eds., *Economic Transition in Africa* (Evanston, Ill.: Northwestern University Press, 1964), Chap. 13.

because they have fallen afoul of local laws and customs. Most often, they have left because of poverty, relative or absolute.

Though the preference for the old ways of life and livelihood must not be exaggerated, for most people in tribal and peasant societies the traditional social organization provided some measure of economic and emotional security. It is thus scarcely surprising that prospective workers may show less than overwhelming enthusiasm for strange pursuits. In many areas, and particularly in Africa, India, and Japan, the industrial worker "keeps one foot" in his village. He may then become a "target worker," [22] with a fixed and definite demand for money. Higher wages may then cause him simply to work less time. Similarly, a high labor turnover may be a manifestation either of a high sensitivity to minute differences in wages or working conditions, or, more probably, of a relatively low involvement in the whole industrial labor market.

Disenchantment with new forms of social organization can lead to withdrawal, hostility, or a conservative reaction on the part of the non-industrial population. Nativist movements and new religions with a distinctly other-worldly emphasis are explainable in these terms.

Nonetheless, a crude shortage of labor is rare. Labor surpluses are common, as demonstrated by demographic calculations and also by the workers seeking employment. Unfortunately, few workers have highly trained skills that are usable, and their presence in the industrial labor market is more often reluctant than enthusiastic.

The most obvious and essential positive incentive is financial. However, the abundance of labor usually leads employers, public or private, to a low-wage policy. Such a policy has negative effects on any attempt to expand effective consumer demand. It may also result in various "vicious circles" with respect to labor productivity and morale. A barely noticeable difference in effective income is unlikely to convert the short-term target worker into a committed worker. At the extreme of low wages, sheer malnutrition can affect productivity. In any situation less extreme, the problem is more psychological—and still real. The poorly paid worker does not usually excel in performance, and poor performance usually confirms the policy of poor pay.

At this point a comment must be made about "economic" versus "non-economic" motives. This sham battle in social scientific literature has had pathetic consequences, among them total confusion of the issues. There are no more purely economic motives than there are purely economic organizations. There are, however, motives of high relevance to the form and level of production and distribution of goods and services.

[22] *Ibid.*

Wherever a developed monetary-market system permits, it may be convenient to weigh the relative appeal of financial and nonfinancial incentives. It must be remembered, however, that the efficacy of financial incentives is always relative to whatever, in the given state of the market, money will buy; this may be as nonmaterial as symphonic concerts or the support of missionaries in far places. It must also be remembered that the combination of all incentives bearing on production and consumption will not equal the total range of human motivation, and could not in a continuing social system that depends upon the performance of all manner of actions that do not move through the market system. At early stages of economic development the "economic" *share* of total human motivation is likely to be small, because of the meagerness of goods and services available through market transactions. Within the economic sphere, however, the monetary orientation is likely to be relatively pure, because the values and any possible nonfinancial rewards of the new productive system have little or no appeal within the traditional value system. Moreover, many nonfinancial rewards and amenities actually do cost the enterprise money; they are very likely to be meager in struggling concerns with low productivity. It follows that through time financial and nonfinancial incentives may be increased simultaneously, and this is indeed one of the dynamic laws of economic growth.

For the earliest phases of economic modernization, one must state the motivational conditions cautiously: an "adequately" motivated labor force. For any substantial continuation and expansion of industrial and related activities, a *committed* labor force is essential.[23]

Commitment involves both the performance of appropriate actions and the acceptance of the normative system that provides their rules and rationale. Whether such full commitment is or can be achieved in a single generation is debatable. The dispute hinges in part on the interpretation of the relative significance of early childhood and adult socialization. The empirical evidence is not very helpful, since the kinds and degrees of incentives capable of quickly capturing loyalties to new productive forms are rarely offered.

Labor surpluses can lead managers and scholars alike to minimize the importance of commitment. But the uncommitted worker is likely to quit or to perform minimally, and to require much supervision. These probabilities have economic costs as well as negative implications for the long-run viability of industrialization measures.

[23] See Holton, "Changing Demand and Consumption," *op. cit.*, also, Clark Kerr *et al.*, *Industrialization and Industrial Man* (Cambridge: Harvard University Press, 1960).

The shortage of skills that may be hidden behind labor surpluses is sharply disclosed in the case of technicians, engineers, accountants, and administrators. These shortages derive not only from poorly equipped educational systems, but also from problems of motivations and occupational choice. Indeed, a number of developing countries have no absolute shortage of people with advanced education—but they are prepared for traditionally honorable occupations rather than those most urgently needed in industrial enterprises. Planned or socialistic economies may attempt to gear educational production to employment demand by using centralized control of schools, and steering students into particular curriculums. However, even these methods do not completely resolve the difficulty of orienting people to occupational achievement in largely unfamiliar fields of work. And the person who is overtrained, relative to actual employment or promotional opportunities, may present motivational problems as serious as the lack of commitment by the untrained.

Many economists consider labor commitment of scant importance as a condition for industrialization. For them the little black box, the magical ingredient of economic growth, is *entrepreneurship*. Whether entrepreneurship is taken in the older sense of risk-taking (with an eye to profits) or the later sense of innovation, attributed to the theories of Schumpeter,[24] economists emphasize the critical importance of this agency of change. No one would deny that innovative leadership is required, whether its proximate goal be profits or nation-building. Feldman and Moore, however, have warned:

The importance of managerial skills . . . should not be exaggerated into a doctrine of "entrepreneurial determinism," which would imply that the notable barriers to effective labor supply of all types could be erased by the comparatively simple expedient of training managers with appropriate leadership and even manipulative talents. The supply of executives and coordinators depends on educational and motivational qualifications. *The same is true for other occupations.*[25]

The psychologist McClelland has argued that economic development depends upon the existence in any population of a substantial proportion of persons with a particular character structure, marked by a high "need-achievement orientation." [26] The economist Hagen has carried this idea

24 Joseph A. Schumpeter, *Capitalism, Socialism, and Democracy,* 3rd ed. (New York: Harper & Row, Publishers, 1950).

25 Moore and Feldman, eds., *op. cit.,* p. 45.

26 David C. McClelland, "The Achievement Motive in Economic Growth," in Hoselitz and Moore, eds., *op. cit.,* Chap. 4, and *The Achieving Society* (Princeton: D. Van Nostrand Co., Inc., 1961).

further by attempting to explain the appearance of such personality types particularly among groups that have suffered withdrawal of status respect.[27]

Almost by definition, economic innovators or those willing to become involved in new economic processes are marginal to the traditional order. Hagen has emphasized the role of "subordinated" groups, but the broader term *marginal* seems more appropriate. Young wives in traditional Chinese households, men in some African matriarchal societies, the Indian caste untouchables, the younger sons in a system of male primogeniture, merchants "unclassifiable" in feudal Japan, dispossessed landlords subsequent to a land reform, foreign enterprisers and the indigenous natives and landless poor everywhere—these are predictably the people who will lead or follow economic innovation. Indeed, it is easier to account for the motivation for change than to account for its occasional or partial success.

Two further warnings are in order, however. The first is technical. McClelland and Hagen are exclusively preoccupied with character formation in early socialization. Since that in turn is mainly the responsibility of parents and particularly of mothers, how do mothers come by their orientation to achievement? We are led, willy-nilly, back to the conclusion that adults must be capable of change as well as children. The other warning is practical. Within a given country, the circumstance that innovation is perpetrated by marginal groups may precisely inhibit general acceptance. The real or imagined benefits must sooner or later have a wider appeal if development is to continue.

The motivational problems discussed so far have centered on productive roles, that is, on the various occupations essential to industrial and related economic activities. However, there are several other aspects of participation in a modernizing economy that are so closely interdependent with occupational roles that they too must be regarded as conditions for development. These include mobility and the acquisition of skills, involvement in a market system, and at least the beginnings of adjustment to new status systems.

The idea of intergenerational or career mobility is alien and revolutionary in most nonindustrial societies. Continuing economic development precisely depends on the motivational acceptance of this idea, and its translation into aspirations for general education and for specific specialized skills. The mere organizational provision of educational facilities is a necessary but not sufficient condition. Even if general education is made compulsory, there is no guarantee that positive orientations

[27] Everett E. Hagen, *On the Theory of Social Change: How Economic Growth Begins* (Homewood, Ill.: Dorsey Press, 1962).

to achievement will be thereby assured. On theoretical grounds the contrary would be true. If the formal agencies of education are to function as transformers of *attitudes*, some affective, emotional links must be established. That is, teachers or other students, parents, lay or religious leaders to whom the student looks for models of behavior and belief may help in linking cognitive with affective learning. To restate, schools or other formal training organizations can indoctrinate, can establish new "traditions," only on the basis of already favorable attitudes or on the basis of emotional bonds supplementary to cognitive instruction.

A part of the motivational framework for economic development depends upon a growing orientation to an exchange economy, and to exchange stripped of part of its archaic social appurtenances. In many underdeveloped areas of the world, the consumer has had a fairly fixed level of demand. In these situations, even if the laborer (or, for that matter, manager or merchant) becomes involved in a monetary system, his demand for money has more or less early limits and is perhaps confined to highly specific products. However, by a process of diffusion that has been little studied and little understood, there is substantial evidence of a growing acceptance of enlarged demand schedules when goods and services are actually available in the market.

The problem, indeed, is often not one of insufficiency of aspiration but rather insufficiency of effective demand owing to low wages and inflated prices. Where labor is in excessive supply, low wages make eminently good economic sense for the individual employer, eminently bad sense for the economy as a whole if an expanding internal market is desired. Even from the individual employer's point of view, cheap labor may turn out to be rather expensive, owing to the vicious circle linking low wages and low productivity. Given any kind of market orientation on the part of workers, uneconomically high wages may be the correct transitional strategy. Thus, minimum wage laws, with governmental subsidy if necessary, may not be as silly as conservative economic doctrine would indicate.

Economic development entails a new system of social placement and differential valuation. Systems of stratification may compete for considerable periods. The point of present relevance is that the change to new economic activities almost inevitably entails a change of most aspects of the "way of life," and the motivational rewards and penalties for the individual will necessarily include his position in the community, the esteem of his friends and acquaintances, and his expectations for himself and his children. The individualizing of incentives implicit in mobility orientations is thus always likely to be tempered by group orientations and collective aspirations. These may be as particular as the "circle" of family and friends, as general as a social class or even the whole nation.

Current empirical research on worker satisfaction and productivity consistently indicates the importance of a sense of participation in decisions and policies. True, these studies have been carried out almost exclusively in "advanced" industrial countries, with educated workers and established industrial traditions. It is probably true, however, that the typically authoritarian character of modern economic administration consistently wastes both energy and talents among those at lower administrative levels, and particularly at the bottom. Occupational associations and labor unions provide one partial answer to this situation, whether accepted by policy formulators or not. There is at least theoretical justification (and some seeming empirical evidence from communist countries and scattered areas elsewhere) [28] for suggesting that the sense of participation would also be an important incentive toward economic development in countries where orderly speed is regarded as of some importance. Do we not now know enough of human motivation to suggest that, since economic development is literally revolutionary anyway, it may be facilitated by sharing responsibilities and giving up sole reliance on contractual and market incentives, or the yet more dismal use of economic and political duress?

The clamor for change began our survey of conditions for industrialization, and the importance of institutionalization of change has been noted along the way. Neither will guarantee success, even if all the other requirements are met, for accident and adversity must be given due debits in a disorderly world. And the costs are bound to be high at best, as they have always been. The sacrifice of time-honored values and practices, and not least the sacrifice of stability itself, must now be made everywhere, and here and there the benefits may not be forthcoming.

---

[28] See, for example, Daniel Lerner *et al.*, *The Passing of Traditional Society: Modernizing the Middle East* (New York: Free Press of Glencoe, Inc., 1958).

The promise of industry is so great in terms of national power and prestige, if not in terms of ordinary human welfare, that industrialization figures prominently in the developmental plans of new nations and of old but retarded ones. But since there is no fixed or stable destination for industrialization, economically advanced countries also continue to foster technological change and economic growth. It is the very instrumental character of industry that belies the foolish notion that industrialization is neutral in its social consequences. Means can scarcely be neutral with respect to ends.

The consequences of industrialization are certain to be more far-reaching than those intended, however. And in an evil, or at least morally ambiguous, world, some of those consequences will certainly represent costs rather than benefits. Were societies as closely integrated as they appear in certain theoretical models, there would be no doubt about the extensity of consequences of a change in so basic a functional sector as economic production. They would be total. Indeed, with such a theoretical model any change would be either "trivial or tragic," [1] that is, a mere aberration or a fundamental alteration of the entire structure. But social systems are not that tightly integrated, and the consequences of structural change not that determinate. In tracing the social

[1] See Wilbert E. Moore, *Social Change* (Englewood Cliffs, N.J.: Prentice-Hall, Inc., 1963), p. 17.

CHAPTER FOUR

# First-Order Consequences

consequences of industrialization we shall attempt to distinguish the required from the probable, the common from the virtually unique. We shall also want to be somewhat attentive to timing, for some short-run consequences may partially reverse later, whereas other changes may require a considerable time to manifest themselves at all.

Industrialization or changes in productive technology are not necessarily simple, homogeneous processes.[2] A small-scale, labor-intensive, decentralized plant that fabricates consumer goods for a strictly local market may not have the same social implications as a large-scale, capital-intensive, urban plant that produces machine tools for the whole country and possibly for export. Although no absolute rule will exactly answer all doubts, a general principle will guide the survey of social implications: Generalize whenever scientifically possible; particularize whenever necessary. In other words, the *particular* variety of industrialization to which social implications are traced may or may not make a difference. The *relevance* of variety should be neither exaggerated nor overlooked.

The same considerations apply to differences in type of economic regime, including the degree of public and private direction and initiative, particular property institutions, and differing forms of political accountability. It may not be possible in fact to generalize about implications without stipulating the economic regime as a condition; but both social science and the transferability of research results to other places will benefit if differences in economic regime are treated as questionable rather than automatic variables. This is a question of fact, not of ideological doctrine. Communist scholars are especially prone to assert differences as compared with capitalism: for example, that technological change invariably benefits workers in communist countries, invariably exploits or injures them in private enterprises. As this is contrary to all evidence, it must be discounted as a limitation on generalization. The difference between social science and irrational ideology consists in the predilection of science for facts.

The more heterogeneous the actual details of social phenomena are, the more "abstract" will be any generalization comparing them. That is, more information is lost in the process of generalization; and more information must be added to progress from the general to the particular —the particular that often concerns not only the policy-maker, but also the careful observer of the peculiar intricacies of social situations.

---

[2] Much of the balance of this chapter is adapted from Wilbert E. Moore, "Industrialization and Social Change," in Bert F. Hoselitz and Wilbert E. Moore, eds., *Industrialization and Society* (Paris and The Hague: UNESCO and Mouton, 1963), Chap. 15, esp. pp. 302-36.

At numerous points in the following pages, the relevance of variable social conditions will be noted, as restricting the richness of the highest level of generalization or, perhaps, precluding that level completely.

A different but related question concerns the interpretation of causal sequences where rapid economic development forms part of a general revolution in political and social structure. Centralized economic and social planning attempts to foresee, implement, or control the various social implications of industrialization. This situation presents difficulties in distinguishing the social consequences of economic transformation per se from the general revolutionary changes that surround the change in economic structure. A paradox is evident here. Many social changes are deliberate rather than unplanned and often unintended consequences. On the other hand, the plans themselves obviously rest upon a kind of theory of necessary and interdependent alterations in social systems—that is, the explicit application of general principles to particular goals and situations. Thus social theory becomes the basis for social action; but, in the process, real differences in both time and social mechanism are introduced as compared with the unplanned changes of the past or the less global planning in essentially democratic or pluralistic societies. That the social theory may be ideological and imposed by force rather than inductive and inviting accommodation does not detract from its operational significance. Again, however, we should not depict differences too starkly. Clearly much of the impetus to the study of economic development and its wider implications has been pragmatic. As connections and consequences begin to get firmly established they are likely to take the taint of utility. Even if terror is not a settled instrument of political policy, something like integrated planning is likely to be, and that will entail attempts to prevent or soften unwanted changes and to foster those that appear most reliable and rewarding. Purpose, after all, is an intrinsic component of human action; as knowledge increases, its utilization for rational control is likely to do so also.

The attempt to "change everything at once" is likely to fail if for no other reasons than the shortage of effective administrative and other resources and the correlative impossibility of perfect predictability and control. The appropriate developmental strategy is likely to be that of "finding the key variables," [3] and those of course are likely to differ in place and time. A comparable problem arises in the discussion of social changes fostered by industrialization. They cannot be discussed simul-

[3] See Wilbert E. Moore, "Problems of Timing, Balance, and Priorities in Development Measures," *Economic Development and Cultural Change*, 2 (January 1954), 239-48.

taneously, yet functional interrelations make any attempt at a serial list somewhat arbitrary.

There is a kind of rationale both for the order of the topics we shall consider and for the topics themselves. Starting from changes in the productive system, the discussion moves through economic, demographic, and ecological changes to transformations in the wider reaches of societies and cultures. Apparent linkages and concurrent effects will be noted as we proceed. For example, a new demand for factory workers will lead to rural-urban migration, if indeed the migration has not already occurred in premature anticipation of employment opportunities. The migration in turn has a direct effect on family structure, since multigenerational and extended kin groups are unlikely to move as a unit, and perhaps an effect on birth rates. On the other hand, some social characteristics are either omitted, because of their hypothetically minimal linkage with economic transformation, or treated in connection with other topics. The resulting organization is not proposed as the only correct one, but as one possibly sensible approach to the genuine complexity of the real world.

## PRODUCTIVE ORGANIZATION

The first, or at least the most apparent, alteration of social systems that accompanies industrialization is in the productive organization itself. If industrialization is viewed narrowly as the multiplication of human effort through the use of inanimate sources of power for production of goods, the resulting changes in human activities become implications or consequences.

In presenting the various aspects of these changes, we shall note first the implications for a "typological" situation of factory or farm mechanization. Then the significance of several ranges of variation will be recorded, since wide variations actually do exist both cross-sectionally and through time or "stage" of industrial development.

### Work Relationships

The mechanization of nonagricultural production (including some forms of food-processing) involves a spatial juxtaposition of workers and fixed machines for daily or continuous operation. This bare, ecological fact has a number of consequences that contrast sharply to those of other productive systems. If the production worker is the point of reference, the consequences may be identified under the general rubrics of relations to machines, to fellow workers, and to supervision or management.

The outstanding characteristic of factory work is the extent to which the timing and sequence of activities are regulated by the machine. Of course, the anthropomorphic view of the machine that is a feature of much of the critical literature on industrialism is to be avoided. Virtually every machine from the textile loom to the high-speed computer has been seen by critics as somehow tainted with evil, an enemy of the subordinated or displaced worker. The pace and rhythm of work are determined partly by machine designers, partly by decisions of management, partly by the interaction of machine characteristics and maintenance work. Yet, for the worker, the proximate impulse does come from the machine. To a point, increased mechanization increases the superordination of the machine by reducing the decisional or optional procedures available to the worker, and especially by shortening the repetitive cycle in both time and distinct motions. Beyond that point complex machines are maneuvered by workers through the use of push buttons or other controls requiring virtually no muscular strength but rather trained judgment, or with various degrees of "automation" the workman monitors an instrument panel and may be required to act only in emergencies. Note also that machines are not self-repairing to say nothing of being self-creating, so that at least some workers have the machine's fate in their power rather than the reverse.

In a factory producing a given type of product, and of specific size and state of mechanization, different employees have quite different relations to machines. Typically, the least skilled workers (for example, sweepers) are not so closely regulated by the machine as are those directly involved with production. The assembly-line worker is more precisely paced by the machine than are materials handlers, although the latter have rather narrow margins of timing. Machine designers, installers, and maintenance men have a more superordinate relation to the machine—as, obviously, do supervisors, executives, salesmen, or accountants.

Short-cycle repetition differentiates factory work from most, but not all, nonindustrial work. Some kinds of agricultural work, and certain types of "gang labor" in road-building and other construction, also involve monotonous routine. The crucial difference is that factory work involves machine-pacing.

A very considerable proportion of the relations among workers is, in the first instance, technologically determined. That is, in a particular technical organization, various kinds of reciprocal and sequential services constitute the workers' required relations. In extreme cases, these relations may require no oral communication at all after each worker has been informed of his duties by a supervisor. Repeated observation demonstrates, however, that continuous, face-to-face relations among limited numbers of workers produce the necessary and almost sufficient conditions for additional interaction. This informal organization may simply supplement and amplify the minimal required interaction; but it is likely to develop codes of conduct somewhat at variance with official expectations.

Despite a host of studies of informal organization, studies that comprise a substantial portion of the research literature of "industrial sociology," [4] our knowledge of the effect of various characteristics of background and setting remains remarkably primitive. Most industrial sociologists assume that informal patterns of interaction established in the work context result in genuine social groups that share various interests and activities both at the work place and out of hours. The evidence on this point, however, is virtually nonexistent. Similarly, it is commonly assumed that informal patterns of interaction not only grow out of the common work experience but also are in some sense intrinsic to it. The observations, however, have been confined almost exclusively to factories in advanced industrial countries where the workers share an established "industrial tradition." Whether new recruits to a novel factory system will find their work experience a sufficient basis of common interest to form informal networks of communications and practices is doubtful. The recruits are likely to be reluctant inhabitants, glad for their employment only because they have no other, more traditionally valued, economic opportunities. Similarly, where the technical organization of production has resulted in overspecialization, work teams or "brigades" that exchange jobs may appear—with or without managerial approval.[5] Their appearance assumes a much greater versatility than in fact prevails among many workers with scant industrial experience.

A paradox thus suggests itself: that informal organization, though contrary to the official structure or at least not part of its plan, will develop spontaneously out of work experience only among workers who have in fact a considerable commitment to work and its associated conventions. This is akin to the point made by Feldman and Moore that organized labor protest is a sign of involvement in the system; the uncommitted worker will normally behave apathetically or quit.[6] He

---

[4] See, for example, the summary provided by Eugene V. Schneider, *Industrial Sociology* (New York: McGraw-Hill Book Company, 1957), Chap. 9, "The Role of the Worker: Social Relations at Work."

[5] See Charles R. Walker and Robert H. Guest, *The Man on the Assembly Line* (Cambridge: Harvard University Press, 1952).

[6] Arnold S. Feldman and Wilbert E. Moore, "The Society," in Moore and Feldman, eds., *Labor Commitment and Social Change in Developing Areas* (New York: Social Science Research Council, 1960), Chap. 4, esp. pp. 69-71.

may on occasion engage in individual acts of protest through sabotage or in very fleeting forms of collective protest such as machine-smashing.

If we broaden somewhat the view of the industrial work force, we can perceive the norms governing relations among workers as constituting a set of closely related ideal prescriptions. The required work relations are supposed to be: (1) functionally specific, that is, confined to the particular duties; (2) impersonal, that is, relating to the jobs or functions and not to the persons performing them; and (3) affectively neutral, that is, demanding neither personal identification nor loyalty.[7] Positions are presumably filled on the basis of merit or competence, and workers may appropriately exhibit deference or accord prestige to those more highly placed than themselves, and esteem superior as opposed to inferior performance for any position. Except as modified by the norms of legitimate authority (which will be discussed presently), the workers' relations with employers are appropriately contractual, and sharply delimited by the terms of the contract.

This normative complex stands in fairly sharp contrast to most of the canons of conduct accepted in nonindustrial societies. Indeed, it is in contradistinction to some necessary institutional characteristics of any society. A purely contractual social order, without affection and without common sentiments and values, does not and could not exist. Accordingly, violations of the austere norms of formal organizations are not remarkable as such—both because other principles of conduct intrude and because the work environment itself provides the potential conditions for modification, as noted with reference to informal organization.

The interesting questions about work relations, particularly in newly developing areas, concern the occasions for compromise with traditional canons of conduct; the effect of these on efficiency; the extent to which such compromises impede full social transformation; and the alternative possibilities for less austere (and, perhaps, more realistic) normative presumptions. In Japan, for example, after decades of industrial expansion, labor recruitment and employment relations are still highly particularistic, especially in the numerous small plants. Wages often reflect seniority only, rather than task or skill.[8]

Insofar as workers are recruited on universalistic criteria—that is, without reference to any previous relationships with each other or with managers—the novel norms may be approximately fulfilled. Paradoxically,

---

[7] See Talcott Parsons, *The Social System* (New York: Free Press of Glencoe, Inc., 1952), esp. pp. 58-67.

[8] See James C. Abegglen, *The Japanese Factory* (New York: Free Press of Glencoe, Inc., 1958).

high interemployer mobility increases the probability of impersonal relations. Yet such mobility, as in Africa and India,[9] is more likely simply to represent an uncommitted and transitory labor force. Situations where the norms of merit recruitment and highly impersonal relationships prevail possibly provide the first of many examples of the typological extreme of the industrial system that occurs early, rather than late, in the sequence of socioeconomic transformation. Later modifications do not re-create the preindustrial society; they do conduce to the development of "relaxed" normative codes within the industrial sphere itself. Where the acceptance of the codes can be assumed, their enforcement may be less severe.

Other ties of varying strength bind the worker to the productive organization, in addition to his relations to the machine and to fellow workers. He has a financial relation, through the payment of his wage or salary. He is likely to be the object of various staff services. Above all, he is subject to a structure of authority. Whether the "ultimate" claim to legitimacy of authority rests on proprietary, delegated political, or even elective political grounds, specialized activities are coordinated and organizational decisions are made by supervisors and managers. This authority is nominally bound by the same restrictions as other interpersonal relations; but it still has a different quality by virtue of its being explicitly graded or hierarchical.

Where workers are also nominally co-owners, as in socialist economies, the principal distinction in actual work relations is in the greater responsibility of workers, through unions or councils, to share in the determination of work standards.[10] The greater sense of participation that this affords the worker carries a price that may be rather high. In such situations independent action for labor protest is not permitted. By participation in the formulation of rules, a participation that may in fact carry little power, the worker may be more nearly helpless against oppression than if the rules are simply imposed by private owners or managers.

Since social inequality is universal, the mere fact of inequality or even of direct authority is not the critical problem in social transformation.

[9] On Africa, see International African Institute, *Social Implications of Industrialization and Urbanization in Africa South of the Sahara* (Paris: UNESCO, 1956); and Wilbert E. Moore, "The Adaptation of African Labor Systems to Social Change," in Melville J. Herskovits and Mitchell Harwitz, eds., *Economic Transition in Africa* (Evanston, Ill.: Northwestern University Press, 1964), Chap. 13. On India, see Morris David Morris, "The Labor Market in India," in Moore and Feldman, eds., *Labor Commitment* . . . , Chap. 10.

[10] See Ralph C. James, "Management in the Soviet Union," in Frederick Harbison and Charles A. Myers, *Management in the Industrial World* (New York: McGraw-Hill Book Company, 1959), Chap. 17.

The problem is that the basis of authority is novel and, ironically, that it is highly restricted. The worker who tries to transfer allegiance from a traditional leader to a plant foreman or superintendent is likely to find that his allegiance is rebuffed in all ways except those relevant to work. Since new employment often means a radical change in way of life both outside and at the work place, the worker may seek a wider and more passive dependency on the employer than that to which the latter is prepared to respond.

Deviations from strictly delimited authority and compromises with the nonindustrial environment are numerous. The outstanding ones involve the special problems posed by foreign managers who use native intermediaries as supervisors. The supervisors may have few talents except being bilingual. They may abuse their positions by being, simultaneously, recruiters for the employers, employment agents for workers seeking jobs, and actual supervisors and disciplinarians. The vicious circle is complete when the foreman freely fires workers for various real or alleged infractions of rules, or gets them to quit by minor acts of terror, and thus enriches himself by promoting high labor turnover.[11]

When the many "cultural" differences between managers and workers are solidified into a policy of systematically excluding indigenous workers from higher positions—an extreme example is the "color bar"—the legitimacy of the system of authority rests in part on technically irrelevant grounds. It is extremely doubtful that such arrangements can endure, chiefly because the equity of the system cannot be sufficiently institutionalized to secure the willing compliance of those barred from promotion and managerial responsibility.

The different reactions to foreign or racially exclusive management provide a series of lessons in the ways that reactions to grievances need not inevitably lead to "ideal" solutions. Certain countries that have long been politically independent, especially in Latin America, have legislatively imposed quotas of native personnel in management. These quotas prevent one kind of discrimination and impose another if qualified native managers are not, in fact, available. Some of the newly independent countries of Asia and Africa have reacted to previous grievances against the metropolitan power and its citizens or racial colleagues by systematically withholding positions of responsibility from them. Again, the policy appears to be emotionally rather than technically founded. Where the color bar still prevails, as it does in some places in Africa, its upholders support political policies and legislation to make inequality official—thus revealing that the supposed "natural" inequality is actually

11 See Wilbert E. Moore, *Industrialization and Labor* (Ithaca, N.Y.: Cornell University Press, 1951), pp. 129-31.

spurious. If colored workers were, indeed, biologically incapable of learning and performing skilled trades, there would be no need to make rules prohibiting them to do so. The exclusion of natives from various responsible positions tends to keep the wage rates for unskilled labor low. However, it is likely to be rather costly on balance, because it results in the inflation of wages and salaries of "superior" workers who are exempted from the need to maintain their superiority against competition.

The discussion of work and authority relationships has revealed a number of ways that typological and ideal patterns are modified in practice. There remains the task of specifying some of the principal modes of variation in the industrial system itself as they are relevant to the organization of work. These may be identified as the type of production, the degree of mechanization, the size or scale of units, and stage in the industrialization sequence. These four sources of variation are interrelated.

The picture of the machine-paced worker best fits the production either of relatively simple and uniform consumer goods (e.g., textiles, clothing, electric lights) or of more complex products with standardized parts and sequential assembly (bicycles and automobiles, watches and weapons). Chemical and metallurgical production is usually either a "batch process," with consequent lengthening of the work cycle, or "continuous flow," with low quantitative labor requirements but with the workers exercising high levels of skill in the manipulation of complex instrument panels, or high levels of responsibility in checking for deviance and failure. Mechanized agriculture chiefly involves mobile machines, as do most forms of mechanized transportation (excluding conveyors and similar methods of handling materials), and clearly involves more machine "mastery" or direction than it does "servitude" on the part of the operator.

In part, then, variations in type of production are variations in appropriate technology. But they are not synonymous. The economics of technical innovation are such that the same or similar products may be produced simultaneously in the same country by techniques invented or introduced as much as fifty years apart. Technical innovation may be related to new products or to standardization and quality control; but a principal incentive for, or at least consequence of, technical innovation has been the substitution of capital for labor, or of machines for men. The degree of mechanization is, accordingly, a major variable to consider in appraising the immediate consequences of industrialization for work organization. To the point of true automation, increased mechanization is likely to be related to short-cycle repetition, highly fractional interaction among workers, and impersonal, distant supervision, because very few matters must be referred to superiors for decision. Automation both substitutes machines for the already mechanized worker and radically changes the character of skill levels and work relationships. (It is interesting to note that mechanization of agriculture may greatly reduce the drudgery of farm work, often without the intervening step of extreme routinization; although other processes, such as harvesting vegetables, may require routine labor comparable to that of the worker on the assembly line.)

Since the course of technological innovation in the most advanced countries has generally been labor-saving, it follows that most of the underdeveloped areas, which are rich in labor and poor in capital, might, on grounds of economic "rationality," import old-fashioned technology. For political and other ideological reasons, they often do not do so. This compression of history thus makes it possible—indeed, necessary—to consider the entire spectrum of technological intensity in appraising the social implications of industrialization in newly developing areas.

The types of work relationships that follow from industrialization vary, not only with the type and degree of technological innovation, but with the closely related variable of size. Size as measured by capital, by units of product, or by labor force is not the same thing, since these are independently variable. But short of the push-button factory, these (and other) measures have a crude correlation.

The ideal norms of workers' relations to machines, to other workers, and to management are more likely to be approximated in large-scale production than in small-scale production. This is partly because of the obvious difficulty of maintaining personal relations with vast numbers of functionally heterogeneous co-workers, and the usual association of impersonal bureaucracy and large scale. It is also because size is rather precisely correlated with specialization of tasks. In a large-scale productive organization, specialization usually greatly exceeds any division of labor known in the nonindustrial economy. This fact has implications for work relations, since it supports a narrow specification of work-relevant interaction.

For this and other reasons, advocates of geographically decentralized, small-scale production units have argued that the transition to an industrial mode of production would be facilitated by avoiding the historic errors (or at least the example) of the West. Japan is commonly cited as a case in point. However, the exploitation of labor, common in early stages of industrialization, is ordinarily exaggerated rather than reduced in such enterprises. We may rephrase this generalization by stating that the intrinsic economic disadvantages of small-scale enterprises are largely borne by workers who not only lack the latitude offered by urban labor markets, but are also entrapped by inappropriate and unrequited loyalties to family-type enterprises.

The picture of the industrial worker is not the portrait of the whole man—this can be painted, if at all, only after tracing his other social involvements and incorporating them. Available data do not demonstrate that the attempt to engage more of the personality in the productive organization itself helps anyone—and perhaps it helps the object of sympathy least of all.

### Organization of Productive Units

The use of industrial technology imposes minimum, but not exact, requirements on the organization of productive units. Some have been noted in our discussion of work relations. Here we are concerned with questions of administration.

Historically, the principles and practices of administrative organizations were evolved chiefly for governmental agencies, both civil and military. They can be applied to industrial organizations because of the common problem of large-scale coordination of highly specialized tasks. Thus, aside from such technical innovations as the many business machines and modes of rapid telecommunications, the links between standard industrial organization and industrial technology are indirect, operating chiefly through the intervening variable of size.

The appropriate size of productive units is a function of various technological and economic considerations—for example, size of markets, transportation costs and facilities, the technological divisibility or indivisibility of capital installations—as well as of social considerations like the availability of competent administrators and the motivational problems of highly formal procedures.

Presupposing that industrial development involves at least some large-scale productive units, we may briefly note some of their leading attributes.

The geometric representation of the hierarchy of authority in administrative organization as a pyramid has a simple arithmetic base. Given a limited span of control (that is, number of direct subordinates) by any manager, the height of the structure (that is, the number of echelons of authority) is directly related to its width or volume (that is, the total personnel). The span of control is a function of the degree of specialization of tasks and of the closeness of supervision or coordination demanded. Thus, an organization composed of relatively homogeneous units may be less high than one with great diversity of tasks. Increasing specialization requires either that administration increase or that greater latitude be allowed to the subordinates in making operating decisions. However the coordinators are selected, and whatever the ultimate source of legitimacy of their authority, there is apparently no other realistic alternative. Administrative coordination could be abolished only if the goals and subgoals of the organization were perfectly established and static, perfectly understood and translated into tasks perfectly performed —a system requiring neither decision nor discipline.

Administrative decisions are regulated by the norm of rationality, even if other criteria of choice are involved. This means that information appropriate to decisions will be sought. Organizations that operate in a complex and variable environment thus, as a rule, develop various staff functions for the expert supply of information. These staff officers perforce impair the "omniscience" of executives; this is one reason that some form of line-staff tension is an endemic characteristic of administrative structures.

Another leading and commonly noted characteristic of large-scale organizations is the complex communication network that necessarily exists. Although pious preachings about "good communications" often imply that "everyone should get the word," this is patent nonsense. If all communications reached all parties, the result would simply be noise. Policies must be elaborated into prescriptions for action appropriate to particular units. Information must be digested and generalized before it is manageable for use in assessment and decision. Relay points and translators must be established throughout the organization. Not only the language, but also the habits of thought and approaches to problems, differ by occupation and by organizational position.

Of course, the standard communication problems are greatly aggravated when even the basic language is not common, and there are radical differences both in level and in type of education.

Perhaps the most common complaint about bureaucracies is directed against their internal regulatory structure. Although a ritualistic and mindless following of rules, regardless of ends or consequences, is a pervasive pathology in administrative structures, the elaborate regulations are essential for organizational operation. Like all norms, bureaucratic rules insure predictability of social behavior. Their special importance in complex organizations arises from the combination of heterogeneous personnel and of the fine specialization of duties. Rules permit cooperation between strangers or even potential enemies. The rules allocate duties to their appropriate places and persons; following them enables one to avoid the twin dangers of underperformance and overperformance. Making the rules independent of particular persons insures organizational continuity, despite the normal expectation of turnover in positions and offices. Finally, the rules establish the basis of discipline—the powers and limits of constituted authority.

The "bureaucratization of the labor force" that is characteristic of all industrialized societies provides transitional problems in developing areas. And it is not simply the uneducated factory recruit, without industrial traditions, for whom this transition is troublesome. Family and class favoritism, personal rather than organizational loyalties, and whimsical administration, are sufficiently common among the elite groups from whom industrial managers are usually drawn to make the establishment of an efficient administration a halting process. This is not just a problem of the prevalence of sin. There are genuine differences in the appropriate values; and these instrumental values (that is, those connected, not with economic development, but with the procedure for getting there) may be among the most difficult to establish.

Much of the industrialization of Japan has taken place in small shops, whose work forces largely consisted of relatives of the owner.[12] In Africa in enterprises under European or other alien control, native workers were not expected to become full-fledged members of the modern productive organization, since it was assumed that they would retain tribal affiliations and partial dependence on the subsistence economy.[13] In India, the long-standing shortage of capital and managerial personnel has led to the establishment of "managing agencies," some of which administer highly diversified business interests with doubtful efficiency but undoubted concentration of economic power.[14] New administrative forms are now being fostered.

The effect of industry on the nonindustrial sectors of the economy is noteworthy. Unless elaborate international trade is involved, an industrial population requires an agricultural surplus, and thus a previous or concomitant reorganization of agriculture. But continued industrialization tends to lead to further technification of agriculture, often with considerably higher productivity per worker. The rapid attainment of these results has been a principal aim of collectivization of agriculture in the Soviet Union and other eastern European countries, and of the "popular communes" in China, which have also linked small-scale and part-time manufacturing to agricultural reorganization. In much of central and southern Africa, an essentially subsistence agriculture persists in tribal areas, supplemented by the money incomes from migratory male workers. As the available labor was by no means fully used in the

[12] See Frederick Harbison, "Management in Japan," in Harbison and Myers, *Management in the Industrial World*, Chap. 13.
[13] See Moore, "The Adaptation of African Labor Systems . . . ," *op. cit.*
[14] See Charles A. Myers, "Management in India," in Harbison and Myers, *Management in the Industrial World*, Chap. 7, esp. pp. 140-43.

situation prior to the appearance of alternatives in wage employment, often it has been possible to compensate for the absence of young males by a reorganization of tasks, with older residents and young women taking on new duties in tillage. The low previous levels of production can thereby be maintained. Nevertheless, it is extremely unlikely that a system that relies on migratory labor to bridge quite disparate economic systems will be stable in the long run. The migratory wage laborers bring back to their native villages various consumer products along with their small monetary savings. Once the villagers adopt the market system they are certain to shift part of their cultivation to products that can be sold; thereafter, to refer to their economic system as one of "subsistence" becomes increasingly improper.

The implementation of modern industrial administration does not resolve all organizational problems. Any administrative organization offers ample opportunities for various pathologies, such as the ritualism already noted, or corruption in the form of substitution of personal for organizational goals. Minimal, rather than optimal, performance is common. Because objectives are often hazy and conflicting rather than clear and ordered, and because appropriate procedures are less than perfectly validated, internal conflicts about such matters as policies, budgets, and jurisdictions are "normal," in both the statistical sense and the theoretical sense.

We have seen that size or scale is a major variable affecting the form of industrial organization, or, at least, its approximation to the pure bureaucratic type. But, even for large-scale organization, it appears doubtful that there actually is one invariably correct mode of management. Three conditioning variables seem especially relevant: the state of technology, the state of the labor force, and the state of environing interests and controls.

The state of technology, which varies according to industry and to economic considerations, has obvious implications for the type of production personnel needed; consequently, it is relevant to the type of supervision needed. Some actual technological innovation—particularly in new, alternative processes of production—may occur in developing areas. Generally, however, "research and development"—which accounts for substantial budgets and personnel in advanced industrial countries— has minimum importance for industrial organizations in new nations. Borrowed technology, with minor adaptations, is common. Though the role of the technologists is ostensibly less, it is in fact crucial, and their influence within new enterprises is usually actually greater than it is in industrialized countries.

Certain recent and contemporary theories of administration have strongly advocated administrative decentralization, the flattening of the structure of authority. The theorists argue that the morale of subordinates will thereby be improved, and that efficiency will be enhanced if decisions are made where problems arise. One principal consequence would be that the managerial role would be purely coordinative, and the coordinator would be less expert (and possibly less valuable) than his subordinates, each at his own specialized functions. Surely, however, such an administrative theory is relative to the state of the labor force actually employed or available for employment. It assumes that a highly centralized and authoritarian administration does not fully utilize the skills of subordinates. Although participation in decisions seems to be a positive inducement to employee commitment and performance, it is not likely to be either efficient or motivationally effective if the decisions (and concomitant responsibilities) are beyond the subordinate's capacities. In fact, the major modification of the standard model of administrative organization in newly developing areas will not be in the direction of loose supervision. Since newly recruited workers will be unskilled and unaccustomed to the rules of complex, coordinated behavior, one must expect that supervisory positions will entail major demands of time and energy for actual instruction and elementary control.

The appropriate principles of administration thus appear to be conditioned by the general and specialized education of employees, their acceptance of the general value and legitimacy of their mode of employment, and the financial and other incentives offered. Where antinative personnel policies have been in effect, and where no attempt has been made to modify and utilize pre-existing craft or managerial skills, talents are clearly wasted or not well utilized. But the major personnel problem in developing areas is the shortage of appropriate skills. This means that the most "modern" theories of administration are not appropriate. Managerial effort will be devoted to education and to giving orders or enforcing discipline—and not to chairing strategy meetings of subordinates.

Finally, the relevance of differences in environmental interests and controls must be noted. The sharpest differences are along the range from strictly free enterprise, through various modes and degrees of centralized planning, to the socialistic control of productive processes. The differences should not be exaggerated, of course. The plant manager in a large multiproduct corporation may occupy a position not radically different from that of the manager of a plant in a socialist state. Moreover, the degrees and channels of influence may differ more than the kinds of influence do. The productive unit must maintain relations with suppliers of materials and components, with sources of capital, with customers or at least channels of distribution, and with administrative agencies of government.

Were all these external relations closely regulated and highly predictable, they could presumably be handled by an experienced administrative group. Rapid change, however, affects not only the technology of production but also most or all of the significant environment. Thus staff specialists, many of them one type or another of "relations experts," are commonly added to the administrative organization. They serve as representatives of the factory or company to various clienteles, and in doing so must also represent their respective constituencies in the councils of administration. If the economic system is highly centralized, these various staff functions may appear in the agencies of the state rather than on the roster of the industrial or commercial establishment. Yet even if policies and procedures are externally determined, at some point they must be communicated to someone who can understand them in the technical sense.

The proliferation of experts may owe more to secular trends in the expansion of knowledge than to the demands of industry as such. Yet once expert (or, sometimes, seemingly expert) knowledge is available, the administrator's quest for rational decision may try to find a use for it.

### ECONOMIC STRUCTURE

Beyond the organization of production itself, industrialization requires a variety of changes in the way an economy is shaped and in the way it operates in conjunction with other elements of social organization. Some of these required changes already have been identified as preconditions: for example, the establishment of a monetary system of exchange, rational cost accounting, communication and transportation networks, and modes of transfer of property. Others are more properly viewed as consequences, and these will engage our attention here: for example, changing occupational structures and labor mobility, savings and investment patterns, the movement of goods and services through the market, and changing patterns of consumption. We shall consider both typical and variable features of economies undergoing industrialization, and attend to trends and sequences of change wherever they can be discerned.

*Occupations*

The outlines of changing occupational distributions are much more easily traced than the details. Industrialization involves the transfer of many workers away from food production (with subsidiary attention to clothing, shelter, and various handicraft products), into manufacturing and services. It is immediately important, however, to distinguish two processes of structural change because of their differing significance for the sequence of development. The first of these processes is *market participation*, the second is *sectoral relocation*.[15]

The significance of market participation as a process of change rests on another distinction: that between the subsistence and commercialized portions of an economy. The subsistence portion does not refer to level of output, though that is likely to be low, but to bases of production and exchange that do not involve a monetary calculus or market. The units of production tend to be small—commonly a familial group—and the participants and the terms of trade tend to be fixed along static, traditional lines. Persons exclusively or primarily engaged in subsistence production are not part of the labor force in any precise sense; and the lack of economic exchange outside the subsistence unit (the village community, for example) makes its productive activity of small significance for the national economy. Though such units may have the potential for supplying food and fiber and surplus workers for economic growth, that is exactly the process of commercialization or market participation that is a necessary first step toward modernization where it has not already occurred.

The measurement or timing of this process of "occupational" change is virtually impossible, even where census or similar data have been collected, since the category "agriculture" is used indiscriminately to refer to subsistence production and to genuinely commercial farm production. Many of the underdeveloped areas of the world have long had a monetary market, even though the major economic effort has been agricultural and much of that production has not moved through the market. China, India, and the Near East are examples of long-standing but somewhat superficial commercialization. Where "tribal" societies have prevailed, however, as in Africa south of the Sahara, the commercialization is recent and very partial as well as superficial. The importance of the initial step from subsistence production to *any* commercialized production is indicated by the estimate that a majority of producers in sub-Saharan Africa are still in the subsistence sector.[16] Such estimates must be approached with caution, for we have already noted in the preceding chapter that migrant laborers returning to their villages are likely to

[15] In addition to the source cited in note 2, this section draws on materials in Wilbert E. Moore, "Changes in Occupational Structures," in Neil J. Smelser and Seymour Martin Lipset, eds., *Social Structure and Social Mobility in Economic Growth* (Chicago: Aldine Press, forthcoming, 1966).

[16] See Moore, "The Adaptation of African Labor Systems . . . ," *op. cit.*

bring back some money or manufactured products, and in the villages some cash crops may be planted in order to join, even if gingerly, the monetary market.

For obvious reasons, the beginnings of labor market participation are likely to be undertaken by young adults, and particularly by males. (Indeed, the opening up of new occupations by new entrants to the labor force is an enduring feature of modernized economies.) Female labor force participation is more strongly affected by differences in family and kinship organization. Where the family persists as a productive unit, as in some types of farming, women are likely to have economic roles poorly recorded in census data except under the rubric of "unpaid family workers." As production (except for self-consumed services) increasingly moves out of the household, the strictly productive role of women generally decreases. Subsequent changes in family patterns, such as limitations on child-bearing, and developments in education whereby the school becomes the daytime custodian of children, make a rising rate of female labor force participation probable.

One of the best-established generalizations concerning changes in occupational distributions associated with economic modernization is the shift from agricultural to nonagricultural activities. This is part of the process called *sectoral relocation,* an awkward but useful term referring to the movement of workers among major types of economic production. Even if economic modernization is heavily concentrated on agriculture and the processing of agricultural products, there will eventually be a substantial movement of workers away from farms. This is caused both by the lower labor demands resulting from rationalized productive techniques and capital equipment in agriculture, and by the many services, including transportation, finance, and distribution, that a commercialized agriculture requires. The prosperous "agricultural" economies of Denmark and New Zealand employ barely one-fifth of the labor force in agriculture.[17] Continued rationalization and technification of agriculture results in substantial occupational specialization within even that productive sector—including highly trained and even professional skills.

Peasant farming that is commercialized—at least to the extent of trading agricultural surpluses for other goods and services—is clearly closer to the urban-industrial economy than is subsistence production. In terms of labor mobility, however, the movement from subsistence production into the labor market is more probable than is the early departure of peasant cultivators. Aside from the differences in relative economic ad-

[17] See Simon Kuznets, *Quantitative Aspects of the Economic Growth of Nations: II. Industrial Distribution of National Product and Labor Force.* Supplement to *Economic Development and Cultural Change,* **5,** 4 (July 1957).

vantages in the two types of mobility, the work organization in tribal societies often offers closer parallels to industrial organization than does family farming.[18] Thus the commercial farmer or agricultural wage-earner who enters manufacturing or some service occupation represents a sectoral relocation, whereas the industrial recruit from a tribal setting combines sectoral relocation and market participation.

The remaining peasant cultivators and their families will not be un-affected by industrialization, however. Although classified as "agricul-turalists," the preindustrial productive units are usually also engaged in handicraft production and part-time trade, at least in marketing their products. Greater economic specialization and the manufacture of con-sumer goods, such as textiles, generally turn the peasant into an agri-culturalist or farmer, strictly speaking.

Various leads and lags can create social problems in the relation be-tween labor supply and demand. Cheap manufactured products may displace handicrafts more rapidly than industrial employment expands, with consequent increases in overt unemployment or hidden unemploy-ment in inefficient family farms. This situation, coupled with a demo-graphic growth of potential workers that is more rapid than the expan-sion of nonagricultural employments, may actually result in a larger *proportion* of the population's being "gainfully occupied" in agriculture. This appears to have happened in India prior to 1950,[19], and may have happened in Pakistan and elsewhere. Generally, however, the extremely rapid rates of urbanization suggest that entrance into marginal *service* activities are more probable than an increase in agricultural proportions. Porters and car-watchers, vendors of tobacco and shoelaces and hawkers of lottery tickets, not to mention beggars, are conspicuous features of the urban scene in the modernizing areas of the world. Thus a change in one historic pattern seems to be occurring. The famous formulation by Colin Clark was to the effect that economic growth is accompanied by a large proportional shift into secondary (manufacturing) production, followed by proportional increases in tertiary (service) production.[20] With the exception of reductions in the proportions of the labor force in domestic service, that trend fits well the experience of the older in-dustrial countries. The shift directly out of agriculture into services now appears to be the predominant trend in most developing areas.

Industrialization, then, implies an increased proportion of workers

[18] See Stanley H. Udy Jr., *Organization of Work: A Comparative Analysis of Pro-duction Among Nonindustrial Peoples* (New Haven: HRAF Press, 1959).

[19] Kuznets, *op. cit.*

[20] Colin Clark, *The Conditions of Economic Progress*, 2nd ed. (London: Macmil-lan & Co., Ltd., 1951), pp. 395-439.

employed in manufacturing and services. As a rule, early industrial establishments tend to be fairly labor-intensive unless economically non-rational investment decisions have been made by installing labor-saving machines. In any event, greater capital-intensity through time means not only a reduction of gross labor inputs per unit of output, but also an *upgrading* of the required skill levels in manufacturing employments. This is the third process of structural change in occupational distributions in the course of economic development.

The long-term upgrading of occupational distributions is associated with technological changes and their implications for man-machine relations. They are also connected with the growing importance of highly educated persons in the administration of enterprises and the operation of complex economic systems. Though the distinction between white-collar or "head" workers and blue-collar or "hand" workers is not very precise, it is clear that the proportion of white-collar workers is closely correlated with other indexes of economic development if countries are compared at a given time, and that the trend in the proportion has been steadily upward in the advanced industrial countries.[21]

The process of upgrading does not benefit all workers equally, of course. Here we must consider a fourth process of structural change in occupations, that of *specialization*. Mechanization and the formation of large-scale units result in the dissolution of some skill combinations, but also the need for other, new ones. Similarly, the growth of knowledge renders some occupations obsolete while demanding a steady proliferation of new specialties. At the extreme of labor displacement in automation, many workers are superseded by machines while new technical and administrative skills are required. Eventually, after a stage—of rather indefinite duration—of labor-intensive manufacturing, industrializing countries may expect a declining proportion of the labor force in all occupations associated with physical production, a shorter work week, and a transfer of workers to various "services." If the displaced workers are to retain their earning and skill levels, adult retraining is likely to be necessary. This is one of a number of situations in which the processes of change seem to come full circle: adult retraining is necessary if industrialization is to start at all, but later the factory workers or their successors require retraining for other useful jobs.

Not all services expand with economic modernization. Domestic servants tend to escape into less menial and more highly rewarded occupations. But many new services appear. Some of these simply represent the transfer of traditional duties and reciprocities to the market or gov-

[21] Data on international comparisons and trends are presented in Moore, "Changes in Occupational Structures," *op. cit.*

ernmental mechanisms. Others are types of activities closely associated with economic production—for example, various financial, clerical, and informational services. Still others reflect the allocation of increased resources to such cherished objectives as health, education, and recreation.

The primary human mechanism that makes changing occupational structures possible is *mobility*. The mobility manifested in shifts among economic sectors indicates nothing about the most common meaning of mobility: namely, status changes between generations or within occupational careers. Broad occupational shifts are not always—even in a "pure" labor market—responses to the lure of greater returns and opportunities (positive status mobility). Inevitably, some movements represent scant improvement and some workers—those technologically displaced, for example—experience "downward" mobility even when the general structure is being upgraded.

Status mobility is a functional necessity for an expanding economy, as our discussion of upgrading has demonstrated. We have also noted in the previous chapter that achievement aspirations are important components of work motivation in modernized systems. Too little ambition results in the failure to seek training and to expend money and effort to secure advancement. Too much ambition results in frustration and either apathy or revolt. No industrial system has uniformly matched aspiration with realization.

The amount of status mobility discerned depends in part on the fineness of measurement—both in the number of gradations taken into account and in the avenues of mobility observed. Thus a simple hands-head division of occupational status may disclose little status mobility, while finer occupational and income gradations may reveal much more.[22] If one concentrates solely on mobility subsequent to entrance to the labor force, one may neglect the crucial sorting process performed by schools prior to this entrance. The educational system is in fact the normal link between generational and career mobility.

Some other aspects of labor mobility are worthy of note. As a general rule, the transferability of skills from one detailed occupation to another decreases with skill levels, because of training time. Thus a considerable amount of genuine occupational mobility may represent slight if any net changes in status; it may simply reflect changing rates of growth of different parts of the economy, as determined by the market or by administrative decision. Because unskilled labor is predominant in early stages of industrialization, its movement between sectors may assume fairly large proportions. The transition from the farm to the factory involves a

---

[22] See S. M. Miller, "Comparative Social Mobility," *Current Sociology,* **9,** 1 (1960).

change of sector, occupation, and employer, but possibly no essential shift in status.

"Lateral" occupational shifts are often made for minute, fictitious, or whimsical reasons, especially by essentially uncommitted industrial recruits. In southern Africa, for example, the fact that workers mill around among employers compounds the difficulties of making a statistical appraisal of the permanent labor force as compared with the temporary, migratory workers.[23]

Status mobility has stirred up great concern among scholars and social critics. Wide status changes, whether generational or within careers, are, and have always been, relatively rare in all societies. High-level managers rarely come from the ranks of production workers. One major reason is the fact that the work experience itself is not an adequate means for acquiring the necessary skills. Educational opportunities for adults to upgrade their skills while employed naturally increase chances of promotion. Such programs are increasingly common in the advanced industrial countries.

The chances for upward mobility are also strongly affected by rates of economic growth. Workers in a declining industry or in a career line for which the demand is expanding less rapidly than the average obviously have poorer chances for marked success than do workers in expanding industries and occupations. The same considerations apply to relative mobility potentials in different countries. There are, of course, elements of risk and chance in career choices, and elements of uncertainty in gearing an existing educational system to meet a somewhat indefinite future demand for trained talent. Precise coordination would require a more sensitive formal and informal training and selective system than any society has achieved or is likely to achieve. Even if by a combination of foresighted action and fortuitous circumstances a relatively good fit were found between aspirations and plans on the one hand and achievements on the other, it would not last long. The processes of structural change in occupational distributions are like most other changes associated with industrialization: they are continuous rather than transitional. The targets keep moving, and that complicates the problem of taking good aim.

### Savings and Investment

According to one doctrine of historical interpretation, economic growth in capitalist countries was accomplished by the exploitation of workers in order to extract profits. But apart from the different dimensions of the

---

[23] See Moore, "The Adaptation of African Labor Systems . . . ," *op. cit.*

demographic problems in developing areas, and the desire for rapid growth, another unique quality in the new nations discourages historical repetition. It seems fairly clear that the effective per capita income *before* the industrial revolution in the West was substantially higher than is characteristic of underdeveloped areas today. Hence, if exploitation is the method of capital accumulation, its relative dimensions must be greater today than in the past.

The desire for speed and centralized coherence in development measures is not, alone, the reason that governmental action is greater in the newly developing areas than it was in the older industrial systems. In the new nations, the state is the only source of power sufficient to extract savings from an economy that provides very low levels of per capita income.

Both socialist and capitalist modes of assembling and directing savings provide for multiple involvements in the economic system. In both systems, one's employment or occupation is the principal source of one's private income. In both, however, the regularly employed worker also is usually an investor, at least in the form of savings bank deposits and government bonds, but the more highly paid workers in capitalist countries may also take risks by stock purchases or other forms of business investments. The investor in a socialist economy may have little or no choice about the dimensions or the direction of his savings. In a capitalist economy he probably has more choice about the dimensions of his savings, but he may well leave their direction to banks, insurance companies, and other financial institutions.

When savings and investments are viewed in the aggregate, that is, for the economy as a whole, there is some basis for expecting a common sequential pattern in the forms of capital growth, though not in the exact timing of the stages. Kuznets' examination of historic trends indicates a progression from emphasis on accumulation of inventories ("savings" in the physical sense of products for later consumption) to a predominance of construction, and thence to producers' equipment such as tools and machines. This sequence is explained by Kuznets as reflecting

the shifts in the impact of technological progress accompanying and underlying modern economic growth—from the season and inventory-demanding agricultural industries to the construction-demanding phases of the emergence of the transportation and public utility network, to the elaborate machinery demanded by more advanced technology.[24]

[24] Simon Kuznets, *Quantitative Aspects of the Economic Growth of Nations: VI. Long-Term Trends in Capital Formation Proportions,* Supplement to *Economic Development and Cultural Change,* 9, 4 (July 1961), 55.

Note that the stages are not sharply marked off from one another, as the sequence relates to changes in the proportions of various forms of capital at successive periods, and thus to changes in the *rates* of growth of one type or another of capital accumulation.

### Distribution and Consumption

Aside from military considerations, the principal aim of economic development is presumably to secure a rising real income per capita. Unless some of this income is reinvested, continuous growth is impossible, and production and therefore income will eventually decline because of the obsolescence of capital equipment. An additional part of national income will be expended for governmental services rather than remaining available to the household consumer. It is that remainder, however, that chiefly determines average and differential levels of living.

Were industrialization to take place in the setting of a "pure" commodity market, in the classical economic sense, the types of goods produced and their relative amounts would be a response to consumer demand. Under the assumption of *consumer sovereignty,* that is, that consumers determine the shape and size of the productive system by their freely exercised preferences, the market mechanism alone would be adequate to relate supply and demand. There is ample historical and contemporary evidence that this mechanism has never existed in pure form, though a few economists would still argue that all departures from that model are less satisfactory than its exclusive use. Clearly, though, industrialization does not require a pure market. Production quotas may be established by administrative decision rather than by guesses at consumer demand. Goods may be rationed, or allocated to different classes of consumers, or sold at different prices to different consumers. But it does appear impossible to operate a large-scale industrialized economy without some variant of a monetary system of exchange.

In the extreme case of production of raw materials for world markets, the expansion of domestic consumption as such does not inevitably foster economic growth. In any moderately balanced economic development, the expansion of demand is the principal excuse and incentive for increased production, even though that demand is in fact predicted or even administratively determined by planning agencies of the state.

In industrialized economies, marketing and distribution systems become very complex, even if they are centrally administered and unencumbered with competitive strategies, advertising, and market prediction. Markets are only one factor considered in locational decisions—and, for many types of production, they are not the critical one. Thus storage facilities, methods of packaging, and an accounting and record-keeping system are all necessary. Since none of these ancillary services is free, they too are subject to pressure for technical innovation that will improve efficiency.

Commerce, or at least distribution, is a major sector of the labor force in all advanced economies. In capitalist economies, there have been discernible tendencies for employment in sales and distribution to rise in relation to actual production.[25] This trend is owing partly to the fact that production has been more mechanized, and partly to the fact that there have been genuine increases in the variety, quality, and convenience of services provided to consumers by distributors.

Commerce also constitutes a major sector of the labor force in many developing areas, but for different reasons. We have already noted that extremely rapid urbanization has resulted in a supply of potential workers who are "marginal" with respect to constructive employment opportunities. The activities of these persons do not represent a genuine increase in commercial services so much as they reflect a minute division of the services rendered among a number of underemployed participants. In nonindustrial economies where commerce has long been established, another stubborn problem in distribution is the preference of merchants for high unit profit on small volume instead of low unit profit on high volume. Until and unless competitive price-cutting occurs, this will seriously retard the expansion of consumer demand.

Differences in historical setting thus defeat the prospects for generalizing about trends in distribution on the basis of allocations of labor. However, we are on somewhat more promising ground for generalization if we consider the *organization* of distribution. Here we may be confident that the expansion of mass markets, often by bringing formerly isolated segments of the population into the market system, will tend to large-scale distributing units. Specialization of goods and services will normally have two organizational consequences: (1) Diversification may take place within distributive organizations where there is a substantial clientele for at least most of the goods and services offered. The department store and American drugstore provide examples. (2) Where the clientele is more limited—as it is for certain luxury products or highly technical equipment—the distributive units are likely to remain small and specialized.

It is also to be noted that the diverse lines of supply in manufacturing, extended in time and space, have their counterparts in distribution. Interdependence of units in the system is simultaneously a principal source of increased productivity and of increased vulnerability to failure in any

[25] See Kuznets, source cited in note 17.

part of the complex mechanism. Assured regularity of supplies is thus a foremost goal of any producer or distributor.

As we turn from distribution to consumption it must first be noted that there is remarkably little precise information about consumer budgetary behavior in any society. Certain broad features can be discerned, however. "Engels' Law," to the effect that the proportion of income spent for food is inversely related to the magnitude of income, was originally stated in terms of cross-sectional income differentials.[26] It can be roughly translated into temporal terms, however. Food, clothing, and shelter are universally the necessities for the consumer, until they are supplied at some acceptable standard. As income increases, these necessities recede in relative importance, and various comforts, conveniences, and luxuries grow in importance. Kuznets presents data showing that the *proportions* of income spent for food in the half-dozen most prosperous countries are little more than half the relative expenditures in an equal number of poorest countries for which data were available—the percentages being 27 per cent and 50 per cent, respectively.[27] Of course, this does not mean that the rich eat less—per capita expenditures for food are nearly five times as high in the wealthy countries as in the poor ones.[28]

To the advantage that textile manufacturing has in using raw materials domestically produced there is added the advantage of potential domestic demand with relatively high priority. As economic development continues, other manufactured goods are added to the consumer's budget. No generalization about the sequence in which new products are adopted seems to hold. Imitative consumption and the ready adoption of high-prestige products have been widely observed. And since the goods are mainly "borrowed"—as are the techniques for their production, if they are locally produced—products need not be adopted in the same order in which they originally appeared in the advanced countries. One fact does stand out: "luxury" items that figure generally or repeatedly in consumer budgets tend quickly to become necessities, and their purchase is no longer really discretionary.

The shift of productive resources from manufacturing to services naturally has its counterpart on the consumption side. The expansion of the variety of services and the proportions of income spent for them are marked in all industrially advanced countries. Some of this is caused by the decline of nonmarket reciprocities and the "movement of services

[26] For reference to the classic work of Ernest Engel, see Carle C. Zimmerman, *Consumption and Standard of Living* (Princeton: D. Van Nostrand Co., Inc., 1936), pp. 24-41.

[27] Simon Kuznets, "Consumption, Industrialization, and Urbanization," in Hoselitz and Moore, eds., *Industrialization and Society*, pp. 99-115.

[28] *Ibid.*, p. 108.

into the market." However, much of it is genuine increase of expenditure for health, education, and experiences, rather than for continuous accumulation of goods. But rising wage levels and expanding alternative employment opportunities tend to make domestic and other essentially menial service progressively more expensive or luxurious.

Comparisons of *average* income and consumption patterns through space and time, which is the effect of dealing with data in units per capita, may conceal radical income inequalities. In fact, income inequality is greater in nonagricultural than in agricultural sectors of the economy, and thus precisely in the principal modernizing portions of developing areas.[29] The lesser income inequality of the most prosperous countries, partly as a result of various public welfare measures, is a fairly recent development. It has not come about by the elimination of poverty, but by a steady expansion of the "middle" sector of income earners—the counterpart of occupational trends previously discussed.

It is a rising level of consumption—initially of goods but eventually also of services—that engages the hopes of the ordinary run of mankind, whatever the additional aspirations of politicians and statesmen. Industrialization will not fulfill those hopes for all, but without it there is hope only for a few.

## DEMOGRAPHIC AND ECOLOGICAL STRUCTURE

Of two major trends in the contemporary world—population growth and urbanization—only one, the "population explosion," seems to qualify in the popular press for the metaphor of noisy change. In view of the clang and clatter of cities, to say nothing of more than incidental violence in the streets, the concept of an urban "explosion" or "revolution" would seem at least equally apt.

Both population growth and the rapid rate of urbanization are connected with industrialization, although in part circuitously and indirectly. A considerable portion of the growth of population is due to the falling mortality rates made possible by improved public health and medical technology, which are in turn largely a consequence of industrial development. The movement to the cities is partly a response to the services and amenities that cities offer as a result of economic modernization, and partly a quest for economic opportunities better than those in rural areas —even if those opportunities are not realistically available.

The implications of industrialization for demographic and ecological

[29] See Simon Kuznets, *Quantitative Aspects of the Economic Growth of Nations: VIII. Distribution of Income by Size,* Supplement to *Economic Development and Cultural Change,* **9,** 2 (January 1963).

structure will be summarized here in fairly broad outlines, without attempting to recapitulate detailed statistical regional information.

It is customary to begin a discussion of the demographic situation of developing areas by referring to the "demographic transition" in the West. The broad empirical generalization is that premodern populations were comparatively stable. High and relatively constant fertility rates were offset by high and variable mortality rates. With modernization, death rates were reduced; and fertility rates were reduced considerably later, with the result that there was rapid transitional growth. The transition is presumably completed when low and relatively constant mortality is matched by low and variable fertility.[30]

A set of explanatory principles has been developed for each of the variables and sequences. These explanations are not all essential for present purposes, but two are of considerable importance. First, it is argued that mortality rates fell before fertility rates because death is always a negative value, whereas fertility is, in most societies, a positive value. Second, it is argued that fertility eventually declines—crudely, this is attributed to industrialization and urbanization; more precisely, it is attributed to the fact that high fertility is inconsistent with aspirations for mobility within single careers and between generations.

The validity of the transition theory as a historical generalization has been increasingly criticized—especially its validity as a model for contemporary developing areas. Its explanation of declining fertility is particularly important. Clearly, knowledge of contraceptive techniques was a relevant but probably not crucial variable. (An apparent diffusion of contraception from upper economic to lower groups, and from urban to rural areas, implies that sheer accessibility of knowledge and contraceptive materials was relevant, however.) The crucial issue involves attitudes toward deliberate fertility control, however achieved. Most reinterpretation of the historical generalization continues to center on some variety of "economic" motivation—for example, avoidance of uneconomically small, fractional agricultural holdings in France; famines and limited land in Ireland; displacement of rural populations by the enclosure laws in England; urban residential congestion and decline of urban child labor in all industrializing countries. In other words, the "mobility" explanation has been challenged as too generalized. By the same token, the possibility

---

[30] See Kingsley Davis, "The Demographic Consequences of Changes in Productive Technology," in International Social Science Council, *Social, Economic and Technological Change: A Theoretical Approach* (Paris, 1958), pp. 193-227.

arises that attitudes conducive to fertility reduction may not have to await massive changes in occupation and styles of life.

Meanwhile, the slowness with which mortality declined in the West need not be recapitulated in the new states. Improved transportation of food from areas of surplus to areas of shortage, improved sanitation, inoculations, the control of disease-bearing insects, all result in very rapid mortality reductions. The fact that fertility has not fallen proportionately and concurrently—indeed, it has not fallen at all in most underdeveloped areas—seems to provide a kind of gross confirmation of at least part of the transition theory.

The initial introduction of contraception may have little effect on aggregate fertility rates, since it may be practiced only by those women who already have "too many" children. Since these are the comparatively more fertile women, they may have higher average fertility rates than women who do not try to limit the sizes of their families.

As the practice of limiting the size of one's family becomes somewhat more widespread, the historical fertility differentials in the West will probably be more or less repeated in the developing areas. That is, urban professional, business, and managerial groups will probably lead in fertility reduction. Consequently, there will be an inverse relation between fertility and indexes of socioeconomic status. This expectation obtains whether one follows some variant of the mobility hypothesis as the attitudinal factor in family limitation, or simply considers the greater exposure of elite groups to Western ideas and practices.

If history approximately repeats itself further, a narrowing of fertility differentials will follow. If and when fertility limitation becomes common, and most child bearing becomes voluntary, a positive relation between income and family size may appear. Children will then become something like consumer goods, to be conspicuously displayed.[31]

Any substantial difference in net reproduction among status or other segments of the population will change their relative proportions through time. They will most probably provide a demographic basis for mobility from one generation to another, since differential fertility makes impossible the precise replication of the demographic shape of the social structure through inheritance.

Family limitation and particular contraceptive techniques are, of course, the subject of much religious controversy. However, it can scarcely be disputed that the rates of actual or potential population growth in the areas attempting modernization threaten to counteract completely or seriously retard the possible rates of economic growth.

---

[31] See Gary S. Becker, "An Economic Analysis of Fertility," in National Bureau of Economic Research, *Demographic and Economic Change in Developed Countries* (Princeton: Princeton University Press, 1960), pp. 209-23.

Another subsidiary part of transition theory that is subject to question is the assumption of the universality of high-fertility values. In at least some countries of the West, it is doubtful that the ideal of the small family was an invention that followed the industrial revolution. Field studies in other areas have indicated that in terms of "ideal size of family," the resistance to family limitation may have been exaggerated. If, however, the desire to limit family size is present, although not very strong, questions of cost and convenience of contraceptives and their mutual acceptability to both spouses assume special significance. One recurrent finding is noteworthy—namely, that males feel a greater enthusiasm for annual child bearing by their wives than do the women themselves.

*Changes in Demographic Composition*

Fairly stable fertility and mortality rates and conditions will result in a population that, as successive birth cohorts are gradually eroded by mortality until all have died, is relatively pyramidal in age structure. Major discontinuities in vital rates or immigration will alter the shape of the age-sex structure. Some of the principal types of alterations relevant to the demographic characteristics of developing areas should be noted.

Improvements in mortality conditions are unlikely to affect the age-specific mortality of all groups equally. (Only very recently has there been any substantial decline of death rates for those over fifty in the most advanced countries.) Where sanitary and other health conditions are very poor, improvements are usually most marked in the reduction of infant mortality rates. These reductions have the maximum effect upon the average expectation of life at birth; in addition, they have other consequences for the average age of populations (they become younger) and for the ratios among the several age groups.

The consequences of changing age compositions may be considered in terms of the ratio of "active" to "dependent" populations. Old-age dependency (i.e., the proportion of the population over sixty-five) is usually higher in advanced countries than in underdeveloped countries. This is not only because more people live longer, but also because the somewhat lower birth rates mean that the very young account for smaller proportions. Youthful dependency, on the other hand, is very much higher in most underdeveloped areas—and more than enough to offset the slight advantage they have in lower old-age dependency.

The unfavorable ratio of active to dependent sectors of the population means that productive segments of the population have greater dependency burdens in areas where productivity is in any event low. It also means that endeavoring to improve the educational facilities for the young in areas where these facilities are meager is relatively more difficult.

Large numbers of children would bolster the demand for all sorts of products, if the means for purchase were available. Similarly, if the children survive to adulthood they add to the effective labor force—if useful employments are available. It is thus understandable that population growth is often viewed as economically favorable in advanced industrial economies at the same time that rapid growth is regretted in the underdeveloped areas.

Sharp short-term changes in either fertility or mortality have long-term demographic consequences—theoretically, through generations. "Bulges" and "hollows" in the age composition of the population, the heritage of past influences, have no necessary relation to current labor force needs or social services and facilities. The fluctuations, in other words, may be off-phase. Thus in industrialized countries with mainly contracepting populations, current variations in fertility may be rather closely correlated with changes in current economic activity, including wage levels and volume of employment. There is no assurance that conditions will remain the same when the children subsequently enter the labor force.[32]

Migratory patterns also have clear effects on age-sex compositions, as migrants are rarely representative of either the area of origin or the area of destination. Thus mining and some industrial centers have greatly disproportionate concentrations of young adult males. Other urban centers show substantial majorities of females, chiefly as a result of clerical and service employments. Radical disproportions in sex ratios usually present problems for "normal" marital and family relationships, as well as for residential patterns, community services, and the like. This leads us to a direct consideration of migratory patterns.

*Migration*

Labor supplies are generally not a decisive consideration in the location of productive enterprises. Other factors in production (raw materials, power, capital) have varying significance for location according to type of production and to conditions of technology and transportation. They all usually have greater deciding weight than labor availability, which is assumed to be fairly unproblematical—potential workers simply respond to employment opportunities by appearing where needed. Moreover, in a free enterprise system at least, labor is the one factor in production that is not assembled at the employer's expense. Migration in response to differences in economic activities and opportunities is, accordingly, a nearly universal characteristic of industrialization.

[32] See John V. Grauman, "Comment" (on paper by Frank W. Notestien) in *Demographic and Economic Change in Developed Countries*, pp. 275-82.

The exceptions to these generalizations are, of course, not insignificant. The self-selected work applicants may not match the employer's skill demands, and thus there must be more positive recruitment or training at the employer's expense. Private economic or public welfare policies may place some types of production, not heavily restricted by other locational considerations (for example, light consumer goods manufacturing), in areas of substantial unemployment or underemployment. When new forms of enterprise are established in an environment totally untouched by a labor market system, workers may *not* simply appear. In Africa, especially, active labor recruitment and transportation were initially linked with such indirectly coercive measures as making taxes payable in cash, which was generally obtainable only by entering employment for wages, as already noted.

Internal and international migration does occur for reasons other than differences in economic opportunity. Although such migration—most of which can be included in the term *refugee*—presents problems of economic assimilation, it is not of primary concern in a summary of the social implications of industrialization.

Migration that is a consequence of differences in economic opportunity, real or imagined, may be conveniently divided into three types: temporary, permanent-voluntary, and administrative transfers.

Temporary labor migration accounts for a substantial volume of movement of people in various parts of the world. One of its general characteristics is that it provides a mode of bridging otherwise separate systems of production. Seasonal migration usually matches labor supplies with the highly uneven demand for manpower in diverse forms of commercialized agriculture. In Africa, commercial farmers hire natives from tribal economies during peak seasons. In both west and east Africa, the employers, as well as the employees, are often indigenous. Seasonal laborers on farms in Uganda and the Sudan come not only from the major labor-supply territory of former Ruanda-Urundi, but also from as far away as French West Africa.[33] Elsewhere, for example, the tea plantations of India, differences in the timing of peak labor demands permit peasant farmers to work for wages on the plantations. Seasonal Italian workers in Argentine agriculture take advantage of the reversal of seasons north and south of the equator. In other instances, the seasonal migrant can find only intermittent and marginal employment off season, a situation common in the United States.

The longer-term, but still actually or nominally temporary, migration has had a considerable history in various forms of indenture. Indian and Malayan descendants of indentured workers exist in many parts of the British Empire, and contractual workers from China were com-

---

[33] See Moore, "The Adaptation of African Labor Systems . . . ," *op. cit.*

mon in southeast Asia and some Pacific islands before World War II. Today, the principal areas utilizing large numbers of annual or longer-term contractual migrants are in Africa. Several million persons take part in migratory movements there, which often involve great distances and elaborate international agreements.

The migratory labor system in Africa links the typical subsistence agriculture of the native village with the demands for unskilled labor in mines, factories, farms, and households. The development of a permanent labor force has been slow, and in some areas it has been actively discouraged as a matter of official policy. Nevertheless, there has been a gradual accretion in urban locations of detribalized natives who are wholly dependent on the commercialized and industrial sectors of the economy for their livelihood. Although the opinions of experts differ, it appears that the migratory labor system in Africa is transitional; the subsistence economy is being slowly eroded by increasing intrusions of monetary exchange, and the native workers will probably not always be content with their marginal status and income.

Another type of temporary migration is of slight statistical significance, but it may have strategic importance in the geographical matching of the supply of and the demand for services. This kind is illustrated by the mobile crew or team, such as operates in some types of construction—it may or may not have a "home base," but is mostly employed at short-term jobs, often widely separated in distance. Although such migratory groups are probably more characteristic of advanced economies, with their elaborate economic specialization, they are not unknown in newly developing areas, where teams of technicians may stay in one place until they complete a project or until local people can complete it.

Much of the migration associated with economic development represents the voluntary movement of workers and their families to places of supposedly greater economic opportunity, and with no intention of return to the place of origin over the short term or perhaps ever. Most of the rapid growth of cities, discussed further in the following section, is attributable to this permanent-voluntary migration.

Statistical data on internal migratory movements are scanty everywhere. For the most part, they must be inferred from the differing growth rates of regions, the growth of cities, and fragmentary information about the directions of migratory flows. Nevertheless, an "economic interpretation" apparently will account for the directions, if not the dimensions, of such migratory movements.

Permanent-voluntary migration does not preclude making repeated moves. Young adults are usually most mobile—if for no other reason than the obvious ones of minimal property and community ties. Men are generally more mobile than women, except where women have gained considerable social and economic independence. Unskilled workers, with their wider transferability by type of industry and occupation—and, probably, their smaller stakes in particular jobs—are usually more mobile than the highly skilled (although the demand for the latter may more frequently bring them competing offers of employment).

The question of selectivity of migrants has wider ramifications. In particular, the quality of rural out-migrants compared with the quality of those who stay behind has been inconclusively debated. One view of the migrant is that as a rule he has superior qualities, including ambition; the concomitant inference is that talent is systematically drained from rural and directed to urban communities. The contrary view is that the migrant is a misfit or even a failure, who moves because either economic or social reasons make it necessary.

Since scattered evidence can be adduced in support of either position, varying conditions must be taken into account and only lower-level generalizations should be attempted. One clearly relevant variable is the accessibility of opportunities. The rural "misfit" may be such precisely because he has talents inappropriate for the opportunities available, which may be limited by systems of hereditary privilege. The qualities and varieties of opportunities may be so different that the ambitious and talented out-migrant is no more a misfit than are some of those who remain behind, but who excel in quite different types of performance or leadership. Finally, several selective processes may operate concurrently. The village boy who has a college education may find no employment suitable to his training in his home town. In the city, he may well be joined by the village scoundrel—who has not only found it healthier to leave the village, but finds that the city offers wider opportunities for his antisocial activities.

The third major type of labor migration is the administrative transfer. Administrative transfers may be quite extensive in controlled economies, with their many restrictions on voluntary transfers. They are of smaller statistical importance, but still of strategic significance, in other areas. Wherever large enterprises have geographically scattered operations, transfers among these operations are probable. There are several causes for these transfers, and in any particular instance more than one may be operating. The most obvious sources of transfers are the establishment of new plants or other operations, or shifts in intensity of operations among existing units when the local sources of appropriate personnel are inadequate. Where different locations are of unequal desirability, even at equivalent ranks and salaries, a temporary tour of duty may serve to soften the differences. Temporary assignments may also serve, deliberately or unconsciously, to minimize local separatism and deviation from prescribed procedures through the periodic breaking up of informal patterns of performance and personal relationships. Finally, temporary and diversified assignments may be used as a training device, making the employee with broadened experience available for broader administrative responsibilities.

Administrative transfers are of minor importance in many newly developing areas—except, possibly, for the succession of foreign administrators. Yet in the United States it is possible to identify residential communities largely composed of such involuntary nomads. And in controlled economies, both workers and managers may be transferred to establish "pioneer" settlements at outposts of what they consider "civilization." The opening of virgin farm lands and of new industrial centers in the Soviet East has resulted in major migratory movements.

In identifying types of migration related to industrialization, we have largely ignored the conventional distinction between internal and international movement. The distinction may be significant chiefly because of the sources of statistical data. National boundaries are real, and they are steadily becoming less traversable by the individual voluntary migrant. Quantitative and qualitative restrictions abound; even countries that are seeking migrants want only certain types. Thus, administered migration, involving official international agreements, is increasingly common. The international migrant may fit any of the three types discussed, but he is more likely to present problems of social assimilation than the native. Even internal migrants pose some problems of assimilation. Where ethnic or other cultural distinctions exist within a national territory, the problems of assimilation in new places of residence may rival those faced by immigrants crossing national frontiers.

*Urbanization*

The crude evidence of rapid urbanization is more apparent to the eye of the world traveler than it is to the eye of the scanner of statistical records. The inadequacy of quantitative data derives not only from the generally poor statistical services in underdeveloped countries, but also to a more pervasive difficulty in administrative definition of the city. In the United States as in Nigeria, in France as in Malaysia, the city as a political entity with clear geographic boundaries is not likely to match the city as a densely settled agglomeration of more or less interdependent residents. The recorded rate of urbanization in cities as administrative units is likely to understate the actual and conspicuous growth of urban complexes.

Although urbanization and industrialization are associated in many ways, they are independently variable. Urbanization can take place without industrialization; at least small-scale industrialization is possible without urban agglomerations. Nevertheless, the economic advantages of concentration and, indeed, congestion form one of the connections between industries and cities. Even the small factory town has social characteristics more similar to those of the city than to those of the rural village. And the city without factories still uses the products of industry for its public purposes just as its residents use manufactured goods for their private purposes.

In developing areas, cities have usually grown at a rate surpassing both the expansion of employment opportunities and the expansion of urban public services. The ecological structure of American and some European cities, consisting of a growing circle of commuters' residences whose value increases with distance from the city center, is not at all the pattern in the burgeoning cities of Asia, Africa, or South America.[34] The cities in the new nations are characterized by suburban slums, where dirt, health hazards, and lack of privacy often are even greater than in the poverty-ridden rural villages.

Why, then, do people migrate to the cities? The answers are speculative more than they are precisely grounded in research. Some, and probably most, of the new migrants undoubtedly overestimated the economic advantages of the city. But that does not account for their staying if there is any way they can leave. However miserable the living conditions, urban public and municipal services are usually superior to those in rural areas. Since the opportunities in the cities have benefited some people in the past—and even some in the present—the misery may be regarded as temporary. The flight from the farm is caused by changed knowledge and aspirations of rural dwellers and, in many instances, by genuinely deteriorating economic opportunities and returns in agriculture.

Rapid urbanization confronts poor countries with serious economic and social difficulties. The demand for houses, streets, water, lights, and sewers necessarily diverts resources from the capital investments that might lead to the very employment opportunities sought, and, eventually, to the income to support expanded urban services. Thus once more we find that the accelerating rate of change in developing areas may actually impede the process of "catching up" economically despite the rich, cumulative stores of technology available.

The growth rates of different urban centers also may not correspond with economic realities. In much of Latin America, the capital cities are growing far more rapidly than provincial cities, which may offer greater opportunities in new enterprises.[35] However, in the capital cities the

[34] See Philip M. Hauser, ed., *Urbanization in Asia and the Far East* (Calcutta: UNESCO, 1957), and *Urbanization in Latin America* (Paris: UNESCO, 1961).
[35] See Hauser, ed., *Urbanization in Latin America, op. cit.*

"cultural" advantages of urban life are more evident, and direct relief or emergency employment measures are more likely. In fact, the national government may derive a major amount of its political power from the economic and political manipulation of the impoverished inhabitants of capital cities.

The overurbanization of principal cities creates the probability of a reverse urban-industrial influence. In a sense, cities may become the cause rather than the effect of industrialization. That is, the aggregation of unemployed and underemployed people who have already broken with rural ties (and traditions?) may conduce to locating plants where the workers are. Some countries have tried, with varying success, to achieve deliberate geographical decentralization of industry. Attempts at rural reconstruction also fare unequally. Village development schemes, in India and elsewhere, have retarded the flight from the land, the rural exodus; but they have not stopped it.[36]

Rapid population growth partly accounts for urbanization, because the absorptive capacity of agriculture is limited, particularly where it is already superintensive. In much of Latin America, however, there are undeveloped agricultural potentials. The limitations there are chiefly those of ownership, capital, transportation, and markets. They tend to have the same consequences as actual land shortage. In much of Africa, the land distribution is very unequal, especially between Europeans and Africans. Traditional modes of cultivation, and stock-grazing on smaller areas with growing populations, have resulted in the deterioration of the absolute as well as the relative carrying capacity of the land. These circumstances alone account for considerable African urbanization, despite official attempts that have been made to retard or prevent it.

Urbanization is not only a demographic and ecological process; it is also an evolving way of life. Some aspects of the tenuous and somewhat discordant "community" that develops in the urban environment are discussed in the following chapter. Here it is important to note that changes in the social structure, initiated in the city, have wider ramifications. Some rural areas are incorporated into metropolitan complexes and lose much of their rural character. With rapid communication and transportation, the isolation and self-sufficiency of villages are steadily eroded. As agriculture becomes more anad more incorporated into the commercial and industrial system, the differences in the qualities of life may become very narrow. The country bumpkin finally disappears from all but the carefully preserved mythology of popular humor. And no amount of nostalgic regret is likely to preserve or restore the qualities of rural life if economic growth persists and proceeds.

[36] See Ward Hunt Goodenough, *Cooperation in Change: An Anthropological Approach to Community Development* (New York: Russell Sage Foundation, 1963).

If we accept the common-sense meaning of *revolution* as rapid, extensive, and fundamental social change, the social implications of industrialization are indeed revolutionary.

Anthropological and sociological analyses usually regard the structural components of societies as being so closely interrelated that a change in any part of the system would have repercussions in all other parts. Indeed, if a model of extreme functional interdependence is adopted, the characteristics of any component of the system should determine the characteristics of all others.

This analytical model, although useful for certain theoretical purposes, is clearly contrary to fact. The integration of societies is often more functional than structural. Functions essential to the survival of societies *are* performed—but by patterns of action (structures) that have considerable variability from one society to another, or from one time to another in the same system. The general functional requirements for the persistence of any society set only very wide limits on the appropriate structural ways of accomplishing those requirements. This may be called the *principle of structural substitutability*, which is the counterpart of the *principle of structural suitability*.

Of course, the specification of the divers component social structures narrows the range of possible variation in other structures. Were there no such relation among

# CHAPTER FIVE

# Reverberations[1]

various aspects of social behavior, the conception of a social *system* would be untenable. The several patterned ways of social behavior would have to be regarded as simply randomly variable with respect to each other. This notion also is contrary to fact, since societies are integrated both by common understandings and values and by a vast network of relationships among structures or patterns of action.

The point of our theoretical discourse is not to deny the functional interdependence of the elements of social systems. Were there no such interdependence, industrialization would have no social implications. However, we are avoiding the endeavor to account for every variant in patterned social behavior by reference to the rest of the social system. In other words, the specification of parts of a social system (say, its characteristic economic organization) delimits possible variation in other parts; but it does not determine their exact form in all details. We may call this the *principle of autonomous variability.*

With these cautionary principles in mind, we can proceed to try to trace the consequences of change in societies. The repercussions of a change in one sector of society depend upon the magnitude of the change—that is, both the degree to which it differs from preceding patterns and the extent to which it is adopted—and upon the mode and amount of its linkage with other aspects of the total society. A major change in art style extensively adopted by artists, for example, may have little effect on the economy, the polity, or social organization. The introduction of money as a medium of exchange may appear initially as a minor alteration of trading patterns, but is likely to be widely adopted and eventually to permeate organizations seemingly far removed from the crass calculations of the market.

The descriptive literature on social change is replete with examples of major consequences of minute changes. Thus a change from wooden to steel hoes or plows has obvious effects on agricultural productivity and on the durability of tools; but it may also degrade the social status of displaced toolmakers, and possibly upset magical rituals associated with the mere technical production and use of the displaced tools. Descriptions like these display the virtuosity of functional analyses at their best, and must not be taken lightly. However, there are myriad minute changes that are not reported, precisely because no such connections and consequences can be traced.

These strictures apply less to the study of industrialization—which is

[1] Most of this chapter is adapted from Wilbert E. Moore, "Industrialization and Social Change," in Bert F. Hoselitz and Wilbert E. Moore, eds., *Industrialization and Society* (Paris and The Hague: UNESCO and Mouton, 1963), Chap. 15, esp. pp. 336-59.

likely to be a major change wherever it occurs, even if it is not extensive —than to the attempt to trace detailed implications of every other feature of social life, implications that may not in fact exist. If the industrial mode of productive organization does become common to all parts of the world, we may realistically anticipate a growing similarity of cultures in a variety of other respects, which this book is in the process of summarizing. We should not, however, expect the resulting patterns of action and systems of beliefs and values to be alike. Indeed, the ways in which they differ become the crucial points of potential conflict.

It will be recalled that the organization of our discussion uses the metaphor of concentric circles, tracing the consequences of industrialization through successive rings out from the center of organized production. An implicit feature of this organization should now be made explicit: the determinateness of the consequences decreases with distance from the center. Thus, more variables intervene between industry and religious beliefs than between industry and the work place. As the linkages become attenuated, there is greater probability of both structural substitutability and of autonomous variability.

## THE OLD ORDER TRANSFORMED

Some types of social organization and aspects of culture are universal in human societies, or nearly so. The family, the residential community or its nomadic equivalent, forms of social differentiation, and religious beliefs if not formally organized religions are among these social and cultural universals. Others, to which we shall give only slight or indirect attention, include language, laws or other rules of conduct, recreational patterns, and various passage rituals marking important changes in social status. The impact of industry on the old social order will engage our attention before we turn to the somewhat novel organizations and cultural characteristics that may also be expected to follow in the wake of modernization.

### Family and Kinship

The ubiquity of the family invites speculative explanation in biological terms, as somehow representing an "instinctive" characteristic of the human species. For such an explanation there is no evidence, and variability in precise patterns makes such an interpretation unlikely. Rather, the family appears to have evolved as a way of combined performance of several functions essential to the biological survival of the species and the social survival of organized human conduct.[2] Whatever

[2] See Kingsley Davis, *Human Society* (New York: The Macmillan Company, 1949), pp. 394-96.

other functions they perform, family and kinship organizations always involve legitimate procreation and the early socialization and social placement of children. Whatever kind and extent of broader kinship systems exist, the nuclear family, composed of parents and immature children, is invariably an identifiable structural unit.

Beyond these generalizations—which are not insignificant—the variety begins. Modes of mate selection, the permissibility of plural unions, the place of residence, the durability of unions, the ways of tracing lineage, and the character of internal role relationships—families differ in these and other ways. The differences are not random with reference to other structural characteristics of their social settings. Since the family always has some economic functions, the variety is related to new forms of productive organization.

Although family and kinship systems are more thoroughly recorded in research literature than almost any other aspect of culture or social structure, the results offer only scattered data on the significance that particular kinship variables and their combinations have for economic modernization. This inadequacy is, in part, a consequence of the inclination of ethnographers to report ideal and traditional kinship systems rather than actual and current patterns. Most discussions of the impact of industry have tended to lump all kinship structures in nonindustrial societies under the single rubric of "extended kinship," in comparison with the "small-family" system of urban-industrial societies. With the aid of that dichotomy, the generalization is commonly accepted that industrialization is an undermining influence on extended kinship systems. This generalization is valid only if the type, degree, and speed of change are subject to question, and it is not assumed that the familial transformation is global and immediate.

The principal cause of the breaking of large kinship organizations is the extensive mobility required by industrialization. This mobility is geographical, involving a concomitant physical separation of kinsmen. It is also social, thus involving the separation of kinsmen in social status and styles of life. The respective fates of adult siblings—to say nothing of cousins—may be very different in competitive economic placement. Perhaps even more damaging to the notions of lineage is the expectation of intergenerational mobility. Hereditary, ascribed social status is widely superseded by status assignment made on the basis of individual qualities and achievements. Despite the justifiable cynicism about the extent of "equality of opportunity" in industrial societies, some intergenerational mobility is essential for the establishment of any industrial system, as well as for the continuous changes in occupational distributions that continuing economic growth requires. The demand that all kinsmen "share and share alike" would set impossible restrictions on an industrial system of labor allocation and mobility.

All this seems clear. But it does not follow that the significance of kinship reciprocities beyond the primary family disappears. "Corporate" kin structures, as integrated economic units and as primary agencies of social control, are not likely to survive.[3] Less formal modes of mutual aid may, and there are many intermediate and transitional situations.

In India, the joint family apparently survives as an operating unit in all ways except residentially; urban workers retain their rural kinship ties.[4] However, this appears to be related to the low general commitment of the industrial worker—a commitment that is low for reasons besides the barrier provided by the kinship system. In China, the traditional extended family was more ideal than actual among peasants and the urban lower classes.[5] In postrevolutionary China a radical reduction of kinship is evident, most clearly in the communes. In Japan, the legal persistence of the traditional family, with male primogeniture, permitted urban employments for daughters and younger sons, but held the kinship unit responsible for their reserve security. Actually, there has been gradual but steady undermining of strict kinship responsibilities, particularly in the cities.

In short, as the social transformations accompanying economic modernization proceed, many kinship relations become permissive rather than obligatory; and the number of situations in which they are at all relevant decreases.

There is a weakness, however, in the institutionalization of the isolated primary family. It is asking a great deal of parents, children, and siblings to demand that they spend years in intimate, affective relations and then, when the children have reached adulthood, treat one another as strangers. The real significance of more distant relatives may or may not be radically reduced. The importance of the principle of descent usually precludes the complete disappearance of the identification of kinsmen as somewhat different from other persons. There are substantial strains and ambiguities in the norms governing kinship obligations in all industrial societies. Since some of these strains are intrinsic, they cannot be considered as simply anachronistic.

The weakening of kinship bonds is one of the principal social costs

[3] See Manning Nash, "Kinship and Voluntary Association," in Wilbert E. Moore and Arnold S. Feldman, eds., *Labor Commitment and Social Change in Developing Areas* (New York: Social Science Research Council, 1960), Chap. 17.

[4] See Bert F. Hoselitz, "The Market Matrix," in Moore and Feldman, eds., *Labor Commitment . . .* , Chap. 12, esp. pp. 227-30.

[5] See Marion J. Levy Jr., *The Family Revolution in Modern China* (Cambridge: Harvard University Press, 1949).

that disturb some thoughtful people in areas undergoing industrialization. Some of these costs appear to be inevitable, unless the productive
system is to be inflexible and highly inefficient. Yet their worries may
have been aggravated by the common failure of scholars to distinguish
more precisely the exact nature and degree of social transformation required by industrialization.

The evidence about particular marriage and kinship variables is even
shakier. Nevertheless, we may hazard certain hypothetical generalizations.

The minimization of parental control has a number of implications,
both for courtship and marriage customs and for the internal structure
of the family. The independence of young adults is quite inconsistent
with any but a voluntary system of mate selection, and with specific
economic transfers such as bride prices and dowries as a part of the
marriage agreement. Similarly, a unilateral descent principle is usually
undermined. It becomes weaker in its status-fixing significance and is
superseded by increasingly bilateral kinship organization. The intensity
of interaction usually increases *within* the primary family as it decreases
with other kinsmen.

If children are to achieve adult independence, the authority of the
father during childhood will be diminished. Since schools provide a
leading agency of social sorting that is largely independent of the family,
children tend to gain an independent status in school. Indeed, the expansion of knowledge and the growth of specialization lead to the situation in which the child knows more than his father about some or many
things. The young are, in any event, much more likely than the adults
to accept novel norms and forms, and thus to challenge the traditional
basis of parental authority. Since age usually loses significance as a
primary basis of adult social placement, the significance of birth order
within the family may also be reduced. Prospective ability may outweigh
seniority as a preferential principle.

Other variables in marital practice also usually change. Plural marriage—never common even where permissible—is likely to decline further,
both because of the economic strains if there is a single, male bread-
winner, and because of increased economic alternatives to marriage as
women change their relative social position. Residence becomes, at least
ideally, neolocal; that is, it becomes separate from either parental family. This is consistent not only with geographical mobility and urban
residential crowding, but also with the social separation of the generations.

Even if the economic position of women is not markedly improved,
their authority within the family is likely to increase, if only because of

the absence of the father. And, since production is no longer a family affair (the "loss of family economic functions"), the mother's duties are usually reduced, so that she may have greater independence of movement and of disposition of time.[6] The loss of her traditional economic and social functions may actually, if temporarily, reduce the relative position of the urban wife. However, greater freedom and alternative economic opportunities for independent employment are likely to compensate for this.

The family only partly "loses" its economic functions. In all industrial economies, the family is the basic unit of consumption; market principles of distribution end at the household door. The shift in marital role relationships usually means that wives have considerable control over deciding purchases for the household, again impairing male dominance.

One common problem engendered by industrialization is the rise of "family disorganization." Of course, if family organization is judged by the traditional standard, the changes made in response to industrialization represent disorganization by definition. By the same token, the persistence of traditional practices may be regarded as antisocial by new standards. But this dismisses the matter too lightly. Deviance from old norms does not automatically involve the development and acceptance of new ones. The loss of traditional controls may result in sexual promiscuity and irregular unions that are contrary to any established institutional order. The reduction of parental authority may simply lead the children to delinquent conduct rather than to self-directed responsible behavior. The greater emphasis on the affective relations between spouses, combined with declining emotional support and social control from outside the immediate family, and the changing status of wives, may produce a great increase in marital conflict. The greater intensity of interaction within the family, and the concomitant emotional strains, are much more important sources of marital instability than is the supposed loss of familial functions.

At least some of these problems are intrinsic to or persistent in the small-family system, and not simply transitional phenomena generated by the confrontation between different systems of values and conduct.

### Community Organization and Social Control

Industry is located somewhere. And whether that location is a long-established town or city, or a rural and possibly uninhabited area, problems in industry-community relations immediately arise. Industry presumably provides new avenues of employment and new sources of

[6] See Wilbert E. Moore, *Man, Time, and Society* (New York: John Wiley & Sons, Inc., 1963), Chap. 4, "The Family."

revenue, both public and private. It may also supply leaders who are capable of supplementing or challenging the leaders in existing communities, and who are almost certain to be major influences in the life of new communities. Some types of production involve difficulties like air and water pollution, noise, unsightly wastes, and various hazards to life and health. The dependence of a community on industry varies according to the relative size and the simplicity or diversity of the economic structure. Yet, once new productive facilities have been established, the community is extremely reluctant to give up the economic advantages of their continuation.

The small mining or industrial town may become essentially an enclave within a predominantly nonindustrial environment. If most of the labor force is recruited locally, many nonindustrial social patterns may persist. This may make it difficult to secure a social transformation adequate for efficient operation, as when workers take jobs temporarily and then leave them to return to farming or when they persist in observing large numbers of traditional holidays.

It is, however, in the industrial city that the problems of community organization appear most starkly. Cities tend to throw into juxtaposition persons of different tribal, regional, or even national origin. Given the importance of language and custom, the residential patterns of cities are likely to be mixtures determined not only by income differences but also by cultural groupings. The sense of community identity or even of interdependence may be thin and rare, particularly among newcomers. It is the rapidity of urbanization that especially strains the capacity of the urban community to "absorb" the migrant even in the bare sense of getting him attached to the network of services, to say nothing of capturing his commitment to collective concerns.

Even without overurbanization—that is, migration to cities in excess of expanding employment opportunities—slums appear to be a nearly universal feature of city life. The fundamental cause of slums is poverty. But ethnic discrimination adds another basis for residential congestion and uneven health standards and public services. Slum clearance usually requires public housing subsidies, a form of income redistribution by governmental action. Similar public action is usually necessary to obviate private prejudice.

Slums are one (but not the only) environmental source of a number of problems of social control in urban communities. Poverty, when mixed with other urban characteristics, engenders acute strains on obedience to formal laws and to informal standards of social conduct.

To many, one of the most appealing features of cities is their anonymous congestion. There are crowds without true social interaction. Segmental and even transitory interaction abounds. So-called *secondary* relationships are nominally features of employment relationships, and are actually characteristic of many others—the teacher and the parent, the public official and the citizen, the landlord and the tenant, and, in extreme degree, the buyer and the seller.

In these circumstances, the maintenance of *primary* social controls is difficult and occasionally impossible. In a "normal" social structure, social codes are internalized early and are constantly reinforced by rewards and punishments (approval and disapproval) from "significant others." Exclusive theoretical concern with early socialization neglects the possibility that new values may be internalized at any time in life; in the same way, it is misleading in its neglect of demoralization. Without the support of family and friends for maintaining moral conduct, and faced with all sorts of conflicting standards and many opportunities for anonymous transgression, the individual may well become a social deviant.

Frustration, value conflicts, and loss of emotional security from significant others are likely to lead to various symptoms of apathy or alienation. Thus alcoholism, drug addiction, and mental disorders have a higher proportional incidence in cities, even after all due allowances have been made for statistical errors.

Crime and juvenile delinquency are also disproportionately urban. The very impersonality of urban life, together with a possible decline in primary social controls, may lead the individual to reject accepted standards of conduct. A cynical, instrumental view of social conduct is conducive to law obedience only when the perceived risks of being detected in transgression are high. Crimes against property are especially marked in cities. Personal violence is, perhaps, no more common than in rural areas, but in the city it is more likely to be paradoxically "impersonal," as an incidental instrument of robbery.

The counterpart of the possible decline of informal social controls and the greater opportunities for deviant behavior is the growth of formal controls in cities. Arrests by the police are substituted for scolding and gossip. At the extreme, the varieties of tolerated behavioral differences and the lack of any apparent common value basis of conduct result in austere, impersonal disapproval of behavior, but not in moral outrage. The efficiency and integrity of the police are questioned, legitimately or not; but personal responsibility for maintaining order and decency is radically reduced.

I have oversimplified in order to illuminate the sources of deviant and antisocial behavior in urban communities. Statistically, conformity with social codes is still the norm. Most people obey most rules most of the time. For many, urban residence is incidental to the maintenance, or constructive adaptation, of customary codes of conduct. Either maintenance or adaptation is difficult where the transition is rapid and the resulting agglomeration brings together people of distinctly heterogeneous social backgrounds.

### Social Differentiation and Inequality

Industrialization inevitably provides a new set of social positions and new criteria of social placement and valuation. At the very least, therefore, it must result in a more complex system of social differentiation. More commonly, it gives rise to *competing systems* of stratification, since its criteria of placement and valuation contrast sharply with traditional modes of assigning status, power, and prestige.[7]

The possible integration of the nonindustrial with the industrial stratification system depends not only on their degree of similarity, but also on the scope, extent, and speed of economic transformation. A highly commercialized economy, with comparatively open competitive opportunities, may set few barriers against new modes of market entry and placement, and it may be able to use simple income tests for some aspects of social valuation. Such was the situation, in varying degrees, before the industrial revolution in the oldest industrial economies. This is not to deny either the short-run or, certainly, the long-run differences, but only to note that competitive placement and financial rewards were not startling innovations. In many developing areas, however, they are.

A slow and limited change may permit considerable adjustment and compromise between the old and the new. One can imagine, and possibly find, a direct transfer of quasi-feudal relations between landlords and tenants to similar relations between factory owners and workers. If the change is sufficiently limited in kind, even rapid alteration of production may be absorbed into the traditional structure—for example, the "familistic" organization of small shop production in Japan. Over the centuries, the caste system of India has been able to adjust to new occupations by forming subcastes; a slow and very limited industrial development could possibly have challenged the caste system less sharply than has actually been the case.

These situations are significant but exceptional. The industrial requirements of merit recruitment, mobility, technical division of labor, and limited authority relationships do not fit well into other systems of social placement.

During early industrialization, few and sharp distinctions in social status emerge. During this stage, the differences in social origin, educa-

[7] See Melvin M. Tumin, "Competing Status Systems," in Moore and Feldman, eds., *Labor Commitment* . . . , Chap. 15.

tion, and power of managers and workers are likely to be widest—even in countries where the status of managers is not that of owners, as in socialist economies. Welfare considerations in those economies may protect the worker from exceptionally harsh bargains, but the lack of competition among employers may give the worker no opportunities for improving his situation. However, the fundamental fact of radical disparity in social position remains.

As industrialization advances, the skills of manual workers become more differentiated, and still more kinds of managers, technicians, and professionals are added to the productive organization. These developments multiply the ranks based on position in the occupational structure. Within a single productive organization, the distinctions may be fairly clear; and the absolute differences in income, for example, may go to greater extremes than in the less complex organization of small factories. The first point to be noted, however, is that these distinctions cannot be meaningfully equated with "class"—unless the "class" system is to duplicate the number of distinct levels; if it does not, the dividing lines are likely to be arbitrary.

This point has been stated here as it obtains in the simplest possible case, where a single and rather clear-cut gradation of occupational positions is available. However, we cannot generalize that such a gradation exists in every industrial system. The kinds and gradations of occupations are frequently somewhat peculiar to the industry, perhaps to the particular firm. The multiplication of occupations and the fact that, except in terms of income (and, less reliably, training time), they are comparable only to a low degree, may heighten the importance of occupational distinctions within the work context, while reducing its validity as an indicator of general social status. In other words, if "difference" means generalized social rank, then an industrial system of occupational allocation results in many distinctions without a difference. Broad income-and-occupational categories may become conventionalized as classes, but without any sensible criteria that precisely determine their number or boundaries.

This, then, becomes the class system of an industrialized society. According to all available evidence, such a society can be made classless only if class is arbitrarily defined as resting upon the private ownership of productive property, and such ownership is then abolished. Differential effective control of productive instruments is not thereby eliminated. Inequality of income and power appear to be at least as great in "socialist" as in "capitalist" economies.

Within this common framework, there are significant variations. These variations include the range of differences in status on a single scale (which may reduce to effective income), and the degree of mobility within careers and between generations,[8] which is related to the degree of equality of opportunity. As opportunity is a multiple and not, except in income terms, a single variable, it entails critical questions about modes of occupational assignment and choice.

Research on these questions has produced crude and fragmentary results, because the instrumentation of research inquiries is difficult, and because the questions themselves have not been correctly identified. Generally speaking, because of the reasons noted above, phrasing the questions in terms of "class" status and mobility dooms the answers to imprecision and low transferable predictability.

The complex organizational structure of industrial societies, and the multiplication of relatively discrete contexts of social action and attitude, necessarily increase the contexts in which stratification or differential valuation is relevant. Economic position provides the best *single* set of variables for determining general social position. But the contexts in which general position is a significant component of social action may be narrowly restricted—even when that position is clearer than it usually is.

Two aspects of the problem of status determination and its predictive consequences must be distinguished clearly. One aspect relates to persons (or families as the normal unit of general social status). The other relates to contexts of action. An industrial system assigns positions and rewards in the economic system in such complexity that precise status is difficult to convert to general status, except in crude and arbitrary generalizations such as those represented in notions of "class." The detailed criteria of status determination in the work context, other than income, will not yield a rank-order scale. At best, they yield "occupational prestige groups," which tend to have a high correlation with income and educational attainments, but with arbitrary boundaries and heterogeneous internal composition. The notion that there is a single scale of occupational prestige that can, without resorting to income criteria, reliably rank all occupations, is pure myth.

This imprecision in the comparison of the general status of persons is intrinsic to an industrial system of occupational divisions. It may be reduced, or rather defined away, in the extreme case of a complete bureaucratization of the labor force under a single, centralized control, with a simple and uniform system of assignment of bureaucratic rank to occupations. This would provide, by administrative fiat, an "occupational status group"—those of equivalent bureaucratic level—but it would not insure that the occupations were comparable in any other respect.

[8] See S. M. Miller, "Comparative Social Mobility," *Current Sociology*, 9, 1 (1960).

Hence, it is extremely difficult to compare the general social status of persons, even if only economic indicators are used. The difficulty is compounded by other criteria of evaluation, since the same person is involved in different, and perhaps many, contexts of action.

In any pattern of behavior or context of social relationships in which varying degrees of "ideal" behavior can be approximated, differential valuation is made of the individuals involved.[9] Indeed, such valuation may be placed on qualities and conditions over which the individual has no control—for example, on seniority, lineage, or ethnic origin. The criteria of social valuation may be highly particular to variable contexts. They may, like the criteria of "race," have repeated or general relevance.

The critical empirical question here is the degree of "status coalescence" or status consistency in a social system as a whole, or differentially for various categories of persons. Economic or occupational criteria can be taken as primary determinants of "general" status; but how predictive are such criteria for social valuation in other contexts? An economic and social system under extreme centralized control is likely to provide greater status consistency in many contexts of life than is a system that permits a great deal of autonomy in organizations and in private lives. This fact is partly due to the probability that formal bureaucratic rank is "carried with" the individual, and partly due to the probability that all or most aspects of social life will be made part of a relatively coherent social plan in a centralized system.

The probability of status inconsistency—or, at least, of independent variability of positional contexts—leads to the possibility that "primary" criteria can be influenced by "secondary" ones. This is readily recognized when ascribed qualities and conditions such as family connections aid or hamper achievement. It can also be discerned in a "reverse" transfer of nonoccupational prestige to enhanced occupational position through family entertaining, community activity, associational memberships, or success in amateur sports.

Although the preceding paragraphs have implied the context of fully industrialized societies, the analysis need not be so delimited. The fact that industrial modes of status allocation in developing societies are set in a context of other criteria of social placement enhances the probability both of status ambiguity in the comparison of persons and of status inconsistency as applied to individuals. And sometimes not even the universal solvent of income will link together one status system or context of evaluation with another.

[9] See Wilbert E. Moore, "But Some Are More Equal Than Others," *American Sociological Review,* **28** (February 1963), 13-18.

*Religious Organization and Beliefs*

Possibly the most outstanding effect that industrialization has on religious organization and belief is *secularization*. At the extreme, secularization involves an active rejection of traditional religion, though not infrequently the process involves the substitution of a new set of essentially religious beliefs, such as communism, for the old ones. In its less extreme forms, secularization involves a reduction of religious control over everyday life, the possible growth of agnostic positions toward theological doctrine, and the substitution of rational for ritual action.

A gradual secularization may be taken as the "normal" effect of economic modernization on religion, with perhaps many isolated skirmishes involving frontal attacks on the religious establishment and many more instances of quiet abandonment of religious beliefs and practices. Yet two other recurrent types of "early" consequences must be noted.

One type of religious manifestation has a close association with rapid social change generated largely under external impact. Pagan cults rarely survive when confronted with one of the great organized religious systems, although the complex religions not uncommonly adopt elements of their simpler predecessors. More significant are the situations where new religions spring up or, more precisely, are invented. In various parts of the world, ranging from the southwest United States to Africa and the South Pacific,[10] new cults have appeared that often involve combinations of Christianity or Islam with old beliefs and practices plus some novel additions. Such cults apparently flourish best among those people who, while exposed to Western religion, goods, and political rule, have not been fully incorporated into a "modernized" social system. These phenomena are interesting in the present context, not as religious aberrations, but as manifestations of the partial rejection of alien influences. They are—in the nonevaluative sense of the word—reactionary.

The religious policies of countries following a communist revolution involve a direct, frontal attack on organized religion, the official espousal of atheism, and the fostering of an essentially religious attachment to the state, the party, the founding heroes, and the current prophets. But communism as a doctrine is also subject to secularization, while older religious systems that offered more meaning to the mysteries of life and death have exhibited hardy survival powers in communist states.

Gradual secularization comes about in part through organizational specialization. As new forms of social activity appear and the close inte-

[10] See Yonina Talmon, "Pursuit of the Millennium: The Relation Between Religious and Social Change," *European Journal of Sociology*, 3, 1 (1962), 125-248.

gration between religion and other elements of traditional social organization declines, the church ceases to pervade the life of the community and becomes a special interest association. The role of the clergy or other religious leaders is restricted, especially in matters now identified as mundane. Religious leadership becomes functionally specific rather than functionally diffuse, as does, usually, the social behavior of the laity. Indifference may be a greater danger than active opposition, since the latter tends to challenge believers to take defensive action.

Aside from direct attacks on religion under communism, secularization is perhaps most potent in the challenge of science. Science has no significance for religious beliefs of a strictly supernatural character—for example, the metaphysical explanation of the meaning of existence, and beliefs in immortality. But almost all concrete religious systems have sacred writings that purport to be partly historical, in the secular sense. More important, most religious systems provide supernatural explanations for empirical events, and claim that supernatural powers may be used to alter the course of such events.

Science may have no enlightenment to offer about the nature of heaven —but it can teach about what causes weather, about the way of getting better crops, and about what keeps boats afloat. In technical social science analysis, a distinction is made between religion and *magic;* the latter refers to the use of nonrational powers and procedures to produce or avoid empirical events. Although the very fact that much of magic is embedded in religious systems gives it a considerable immunity to challenge, it does not survive rational challenges over the long run. Since magic is vulnerable, its union with religion implies that the strong defense of magical practices incurs the risk of general alienation from religious doctrines.

The universal function of magic is to eke out the difference between rational prediction and control, on the one hand, and the felt need for control on the other. As rational techniques are improved, they become accepted as more efficacious than magical ones. Nevertheless, the uncertainties of human existence are, and are likely to remain, such as to provide opportunities for old and new magic. The derogation of magic as "superstition" indicates the relative success of rational orientations; but the persistence of magic despite derogation must also be noted. The secular attitude is not wholly satisfactory for confronting many of life's problems. However, it is likely to spread to many aspects of human activity, as part of the habits of thought encouraged by technical change and problem-solving orientations. In the process of this diffusion, some established religious rituals will either be modified or fall into disuse.

## THE NEW ORDER EVOLVING

Novelty does occur in human affairs, despite world-weary protestations that there is nothing new under the sun. Some of the changes wrought by economic development are sufficiently different in organization and functional significance that they may be properly regarded as elements of a new social order, an order that will continue to change as economic growth continues.

### Education and Science

Although factory production or commercialized agriculture may be introduced with an illiterate and largely unskilled labor force for manual operations, at least a minority must have higher education and technical skills. As industrial or agricultural operations become more complex, rising levels of general education are needed.

Literacy is by no means common in underdeveloped areas, and technical skills are often in very short supply. The expansion of education is both a cause and a consequence of economic development. Neither the historic record in older industrial countries nor the more recent record in developing areas has been subjected to the kind of searching, quantitative analysis that would make possible a more precise statement of the relative importance of cause and consequence or of the rates and sequences of change.

Because these basic questions have not been answered, there are moot questions of social strategy involved in formulating educational policy for developing areas. The possibility of utilizing abundant unskilled labor—even if wastefully and with outmoded technology—leads some experts to emphasize the initial provision of technical, professional, and administrative skills. Others argue that such skills can be imported or that people can be trained abroad; that available resources should be used for the widest possible extension of general education.[11]

A system of universal education provides a more effective system of identifying, sorting, and cultivating latent talents than any alternative system of social selection. The uneducated are doomed to poorly paid and low-status jobs, whatever their potential talents. The proponents of mass education add political and social considerations to the economic ones. Full participation in community or national life is scarcely possible for the illiterate workingman or housewife.

[11] See C. Arnold Anderson and Mary Jean Bowman, eds., *Education in the Early Stages of Development* (Chicago: Aldine Press, 1965), esp. Part IV, "Human Factor Preconditions, the Timing of Emergence, and the Pace of Change."

In a developing area, the role of the school in providing literacy—
and, for some, more highly trained skills—is supplemented by its effectiveness in forming achievement orientations and an approach to situations very different from those of most traditional cultures. Secular
education encourages a rational, problem-solving habit of mind, rather
than an unquestioning acceptance or explanation in terms of nonrational categories.[12] This is perhaps the crucial difference between workers
with industrial traditions and workers without them.

The correlation of educational supply with manpower demands is not
perfect anywhere. Schools are imperfectly matched with the current
occupational needs, and occupational choices are made on grounds besides objective rewards and opportunities. In addition, the schools must
train people for an uncertain future. This leads to the troublesome
issues involved in general versus specialized training. The latter may
be more quickly and exactly related to current manpower needs; but it
is vulnerable to obsolescence if changing technology, markets, or administrative policies remove the need for the skill. General education
to a fairly high level presumably lays the foundation for short specific
training in many fields and for relatively easy retraining as needs and
opportunities change; but it is always in danger of being regarded as
useless for any specific purpose.

Because educational curriculums and school graduates are incompletely matched with manpower needs in the economy, the employer,
whether public or private, must devote some organizational resources to
personnel training. The short supply and often the poor quality of the
output of the schools in developing areas make on-the-job training even
more essential. It is also more difficult, since the supply of qualified
managerial personnel is severely enough limited before training is added
to supervisory functions.

The pursuit of pure science in underdeveloped areas is difficult for
several reasons: the limited quantity and quality of appropriately educated people; the limited resources available for scientific work; and the
urgent need for applied science in current technological and other problems. The last is by no means least. In some centers of old cultures,
long traditions of scholarship in the humanities are currently preserved
with pride. No one requires humanistic scholars to be practical. But in
the natural and social sciences, the need to utilize scarce intellectual resources for the solution of urgent problems discourages attempts to
pursue possibly useless knowledge. This situation is regretted by the
international brotherhood of scholars; but it is likely to continue as long

---

[12] See Wilbert E. Moore, *Social Change* (Englewood Cliffs, N.J.: Prentice-Hall,
Inc., 1963), pp. 110-11.

as the countries are poor and are borrowers, rather than inventors, of knowledge and techniques. The line between "pure" and "applied" is not absolute; important additions to abstract knowledge may result from action-oriented research. However, these essentially accidental contributions are not likely to loom large in the general progress of knowledge.

It is tempting to assert that the long-term course of industrialization results in a steadily increased demand for, and investment in, high-level education and its manifestations in science and technology. The generalization matches the course of education and science in advanced industrial countries, but it would be extremely difficult to disentangle the effects of economic development as such and the effects of military requirements and policies. And yet it is also to be noted that in the modern world not only may military demands shape the development of technology, but also that military service may be a principal agency of technical education where the schools have not produced persons with appropriate technical skills.

### Communication and Popular Culture

Perhaps the single most important technical product of modern industry, in terms of the number of people directly affected in their everyday lives, is the radio. Very few areas of the world are not reached by radio broadcasts—if not over private household sets, then over public loudspeakers in village squares. Newspapers depend upon a considerable technical organization and a literate public. Television is too expensive to reach most people in underdeveloped areas. Radio, however, has neither handicap. For many, it provides their first and only substantial contact with events and ideas in the world outside their village. The movies have had a somewhat similar impact, but with a more restricted diffusion.

Economic development tends, sooner or later, to bring all areas and sectors of production into a national, if not international, economic network. The process may be slow and uneven, however. The mass media of communication, and particularly radio broadcasts, supply the technical basis for the formation of a national public and a widespread, if passive, participation in political events and policies, popular drama, and music.

The extent to which radio standardizes political attitudes or musical forms, even when broadcasting is governmentally and centrally controlled, is still debatable. Radio clearly serves most reliably simply in communicating information. In many areas, its chief additional effect may be to make villagers arrive at the rather revolutionary realization that village life is not isolated and autonomous. It is possible that the development of a mass or popular culture may be rather rapid in developing areas. Thus the eventual outcome of a long chain of technical changes in communication, as a consequence of industrialization, may well precede any substantial economic transformation in the underdeveloped areas. We have, then, a further example not only of accelerating rates of change but also of an altered sequence.

It is precisely the standardization and possible degradation of ideas and tastes that most concern the critics of mass culture. In some instances, a distinctly snobbish attitude is discernible: popularity is equated to vulgarity, even if there has been no change in, say, the art forms involved. Thus musical classics on radio or on records are regarded as having lost quality by the mere fact of having wider circulation.

The debate is a little hard to transplant to impoverished areas that do not have a national market for best-selling books or equipment for playing high-fidelity recordings; yet, in slightly altered form, the policy debate does occur. One of the worries about the supposed standardizing consequences of industrialization concerns the charge that much of the cultural variety that existed within and among nonindustrial cultures will be lost. The radio and the movies are considered as substituting passive entertainment for traditional dances, fiestas, and other modes of recreation and expression.

For reasons not directly linked to industrialization as such, the alarm would be inappropriate even if it were valid to assume that new entertainments are uniformly inferior to old. The growth of nationalistic sentiment that accompanies programs of economic development often leads to the preservation, restoration, or adaptation of elements of folk culture. Nor is this necessarily anachronistic. Esthetic and expressive forms and canons are, of all aspects of culture, least intimately connected with other elements in social systems.[13] In other words, their functional autonomy is relatively high. The essential truth of this assertion is not damaged by the recognition that preservation of exotic crafts and rituals may be encouraged as a tourist attraction. The motives of the participants may be mixed; but it does not follow that the cultural forms are radically transformed by commercial considerations.

Folk customs may be preserved, or only partially lost and modified, in cultural enclaves within burgeoning cities. All experience to date evinces their hardy survival power, even when they confront the undeniable standardizing influences and the growth of commercialized, often passive recreation (for example, the movies and spectator sports).

13 *Ibid.*, pp. 75-76.

For some frustrated, footloose, and discontented urban dwellers, escapes may go to antisocial extremes or lead to personal disorganization, as illustrated by the bums in many large cities. Gambling may introduce pleasant uncertainty into lives otherwise all too predictable and routine.

One matter that excites the attention of social critics in advanced countries has a qualitatively different significance in underdeveloped areas—the problem of leisure. Leisure *is* a problem for the unemployed and underemployed. But their principal problem is to gain an adequate income, not to decide what to do with their involuntary freedom. The problem of leisure in advanced countries is what use to make of time that is a consequence of productive efficiency and prosperity—that is, one's nonworking hours while one is "fully" employed.[14]

It would be too glib to say that the people in many underdeveloped areas wish that they had this problem. Working hours may in fact be shortened—not because of the high productive efficiency achieved, but as a measure to spread employment. Socialist states try to find devices to assure full employment, and they also devote a great deal of attention explicitly to providing leisure activities, ranging from work brigades to doctrinal study groups. And, where leisure is less organized and controlled, the urban environment and the products of industry afford opportunities for adult self-directed recreation. The problem is often one of attitude, not of opportunity.

### Interest Groups and Associations

The multiplication of organizations is one clear consequence of industrialization. Some organizations, like unions and occupational groups, are directly related to new forms of work. Others represent new involvements in national political life. Still others are organized manifestations of the potential multitude of interests that become involved when the notion of deliberate social action has taken hold. Finally, associations may simply reflect the common expressive and recreational interests of their members. In a sense, they all represent substitutes for the multifunctional structures that constituted the traditional basis of village life.

The industrial system of production introduces new occupations and new forms of organization. These are inevitably accompanied by new tensions in work relations, new bases of distinction and allegiance. At least four possible bases of identification by workers are potentially operative in industrial and related employments.[15] (1) The worker may identify with the employer and thus become a "loyal" employee. (2) By

[14] See Moore, *Man, Time and Society*, pp. 32-39.
[15] See Wilbert E. Moore, "Notes for a General Theory of Labor Organization," *Industrial and Labor Relations Review*, 13 (April 1960), 387-97.

doing so, he may also identify with the industry or sector of the economy —for example, when the new recruit becomes committed to the modern, as opposed to the subsistence, sector of the economy; to factory, rather than agricultural, wage-labor; to steel, instead of aluminum, for construction (because his skills and livelihood are bound up with the market for steel). (3) As an employee—as distinct from an employer or a manager—he may identify with other employees of similar status. (4) As a worker in a particular occupation, he may identify with people who have similar training and skills and, possibly, similar economic interests.

It is an academic or ideological prejudice that any one of these interests is more "normal" than another. Since they are all actually or potentially operative, strains among them as competing bases of allegiance are intrinsic, not abnormal. Generalization about the "predominant" form of interest-group organization is hazardous unless other conditions are stipulated. If union organization and membership are more or less voluntary, and the bases of allegiance are somewhat competitive, then something approximating the following sequence evolves.[16] The new recruit is usually not interested in unions at all. Union membership is indicative of at least partial commitment to the new forms of labor. Early unions are likely to be composed exclusively of skilled craft workers, because of their strategic power and greater sophistication—or, if the unions are organized on a broader basis, they are led by such workers. The appearance of status-conscious industrial or general unions manifests a realization of the actual disparities of status and career opportunities for managers and workers.

The broadly based union, however, does not dispel other bases of allegiance and division—especially those that revolve around distinct occupational interests. The steady increase of specialization and the growth of technical and professional groups combine to undermine the common status interests and to impel occupational organization. These organizations either form cliques and parties within a general union or constitute separate organizations. In either event, coalitions among them may operate for particular purposes but prove unstable as interests and events shift in a dynamic society.

In socialist states, unions are controlled; rival unions, whether based on competing jurisdictional claims or on competing principles (craft versus industrial) are not ordinarily tolerated. In these circumstances, the strike is not available to unions as a bargaining device. However, unions apparently retain functions of collective representation and protest. Centralized control is tightest at the national political level. Locally, the

[16] *Ibid.* See also Clark Kerr *et al., Industrialization and Industrial Man* (Cambridge: Harvard University Press, 1960).

managerial organization, the political organization, and the union are discrete, if interdependent agencies. Some leverage on the system of social organization is thus possible. The official powers of the respective organizations and their jurisdictions are not always clear, and actions may appear to be capricious, as Smelser notes.[17] At the same time that labor organization is expected to participate actively in technical innovation and improved worker productivity, it also has some duty to represent workers' grievances. In these circumstances, Zawodny observes that the protest function often operates informally.[18]

Unions in underdeveloped areas are sometimes characterized as agencies for the "management of protest." [19] That management may be incomplete if freedom of association does not exist, or if the avenues of legal protest are very narrowly restricted or totally prohibited. The prominent political interests and activities evinced by unions in many countries seem to derive from two sources. One is the fact that party and other kinds of political participation may be incompletely developed —indeed, the franchise may be denied by various kinds of voting restrictions. The other source is that the "economic" power of unions must, sooner or later, rest upon their political legitimacy. Until that legitimacy has been established by legislation, the employer's position is buttressed by courts, administrative agencies, and the police.

Membership in a union does not necessarily imply rejection of "the system." The uncommitted worker does not join in labor protest, except under pressure from his fellows. An industrial system institutionalizes conflicts and tensions; it does not eliminate them.

Unions, then, become agencies of change. Viewed restrictively or negatively, they cushion the impact of change or alter the conditions under which change occurs. But in at least some instances, labor organizations take the lead in fostering change, through acting as labor recruiters for new industrial employments and even through exhibiting active concern for the living conditions in industrial communities and for working conditions in industrial plants. Mexico provides vivid illustrations of labor unions that participate actively—and impel their members to do so—in social transformation though resisting some features of employment policies.[20]

Political participation may be organized around either unions and

---

[17] Neil J. Smelser, *The Sociology of Economic Life* (Englewood Cliffs, N.J.: Prentice-Hall, Inc., 1963), p. 49.

[18] Janusz Zawodny, "Grievance Procedures in Soviet Factories," *Industrial and Labor Relations Review*, 10 (Winter, 1956-57), 553.

[19] Kerr *et al., op. cit.,* esp. Chap. 8, "The Workers: Impact and Response."

[20] See Wilbert E. Moore, *Industrialization and Labor* (Ithaca, N.Y.: Cornell University Press, 1951), pp. 239-40.

other occupational groups or a variety of other interests and loyalties. A single-party system seeks to minimize political division, but not political participation. Most totalitarian regimes rest on wide, though stringently controlled, participation.

The relationship between economic development and increased political participation is less apparent than some other social consequences, but the connection can still be discerned. The tensions produced by widespread, fundamental social dislocation engender efforts to control or modify the situation through political action. If legal political action is thwarted, the activity then becomes criminal or rebellious. Like the union, the political party may become an agency of protest—effective or impotent. When linked to anticolonial or other nationalistic movements, the political organization mobilizes sentiment and action on behalf of governmental policies, and incidentally diverts criticism from the internal weaknesses and strains in the social order.

The economic and cultural interests that may form the basis of political action are very diverse in *any* society. A single-party or two-party system does not dispel such divisive interests; the interests simply necessitate more elaborate compromises and coalitions to be formed within the party, rather than between parties, in order for the party to be able to legislate and govern.

As all sorts of social functions become conducted by specialized organizations—like welfare agencies, hospitals, schools, and consumer cooperatives—voluntary associations are frequently formed to promote, support, and control those organizations. Associations may also be formed to promote or prevent a host of undesired actions. The most striking common feature of the many associations that are likely to emerge with urban industrialization is the idea that purposive social action is possible and appropriate. This idea is comparatively uncommon in traditionally organized societies. Although the heady idea of social betterment or prevention often generates a multitude of rather ineffectual groups, their members do at least manifestly accept a rather revolutionary change in the proper relation of the individual to the social order.

Studies of associations and their members are not far advanced anywhere. Obviously, a major conditioning factor is the legal code—that is, whether freedom of association is broadly interpreted or virtually nonexistent.[21] A closely related condition is the extent to which some associations, like political parties or unions, are genuinely multifunctional, which quality avoids the degree of multiplication of separate organizations observable in some countries.

[21] See Arnold M. Rose, *Sociology* (New York: Alfred A. Knopf, Inc., 1956), Chap. 10, "Voluntary Associations," esp. Part A, "Conditions for Development," pp. 305-9.

Where freedom of association is extensive and membership is largely voluntary, patterns of differential participation recur. The "joiners," or "good organization people," are generally not those who ostensibly would benefit most by social action or seem to be most in need of being diverted after frustrating routines at work. Rather, associations are usually composed of successful, often upwardly mobile, elements in the population. The persons who apparently derive high work satisfactions from their jobs also seem to have time and energy for other organized activities.[22] Differential participation can be understood not in terms of the range from frustration to success, but in terms of the range from apathy to positive self-confidence.

In a subtle sense, freedom of association may be inconsistent with voluntary participation. The interests promoted by an association may have negative consequences for others. Therefore, once an interest group has become active, its collective effort may call forth the formation of associations to protect the interests it threatens. Thus the freedom not to join interest groups may be exercised only at the risk of losing ground, relatively or absolutely. This is as true of associations to promote, say, wild-life preservation as it is of the more obvious case of the partial but economically successful union organizations that result in the relative deterioration of the economic positions of workers who are not organized.

We shall now consider the associational counterpart of popular culture. Fraternal associations, although they often have political or religious overtones, probably serve more nearly recreational functions, as do amateur sport organizations, musical groups, collectors' societies, and the like. One encounters differential patterns of participation, partly caused by the actual costs (dues, equipment, financial resources for collecting). It is also probable, however, that the apathy and discontent felt by poorly paid and marginal workers are general attitudes that do not conduce to their involvement in "cultivated" leisure activities.

A caution should be given here. Its flavor is conveyed by the aphorism "The pub is the poor man's club." Some of the differential participation may be a statistical manifestation of the fact that formal associations have constitutions, bylaws, and membership lists. Nonjoiners may find their recreation in genuine groups that lack formal trappings. Time-budgets of behavior would give more precise dimensions to our knowledge of voluntary social activity—but that research instrument has never been adequately refined or used.[23]

---

[22] See Moore, *Man, Time, and Society,* Chap. 6, "Voluntary Associations."
[23] *Ibid.*

The historical and contemporary variety of state organization in industrialized societies manifests the fact that there is considerable independent variation between economic and political organization. Indeed, at first glance, it seems impossible to make any generalization concerning the political implications of industrialization. However, careful scrutiny discovers some common elements and characterisitcs.

These common elements are more readily identifiable in the administrative than in the strictly political structure of the state. All contemporary states use a similar administrative structure for carrying out public functions—the "bureaucratic organization." We need not recapitulate here the essential features of bureaucratic organizations, in terms of gradations of authority, the matching of power and responsibility, clear-cut functional specialization, merit placement, and so forth. It seems unlikely that any other mode of conducting regular public functions could achieve the required reliability and accountability of action.

Administrative structures differ in detail, and in their relative magnitudes in the society as a whole. Specific agencies and their relative importances vary from one country to another, as does the mode of relationship between administrative and political authorities. Experts agree that the efficiency and reliability of administration are greatly impaired if it is not established as a permanent civil service, rather than being staffed through patronage and subject to detailed political interference or turnover. Similarly, efficiency is presumably impaired by any form of particularistic placement, such as nepotism, even if not politically inspired. And corruption—in the technical sense, that is, the substitution of individual for organizational ends—is a potential problem in all bureaucracies. Corruption may range from a conflict of interest between the official's public responsibilities and his private, otherwise legitimate, interests, to outright graft. If personal moral standards are not taken into account, graft can be regarded as usually related to slow, complicated, and unreliable administrative action and procedures.

Modern public administration is fairly novel in some of the developing areas; and it is not surprising that it is often judged to be inefficient, if not corrupt. The difficulty of securing technically qualified administrators represents part of the problem; and competing demands from commerce and industry will do nothing to improve that situation. However, the acceptance of a somewhat novel normative system is also involved. This acceptance requires either widespread changes in individual attitudes, or the imposition of exceptionally rigorous discipline "from the top down."

The connection between the economy and the polity can best be approached in terms of minimum and maximum degrees of state regulation of economic activities. The minimum is apparently determined by the necessity of preserving order, enforcing institutional rules (including those relating to various business practices), and the public provision of financial and fiscal responsibility. Even such a minimum presupposes the development of efficient public administration.

The maximum effective control by the state need not be total. The planned and controlled integration of an entire complex economy may have to leave margins of uncertainty and individual choice. One reason for this incomplete control is the impossibility of having perfect advance knowledge of the outcome of the interaction of many, partially uncontrolled variables. In addition, the administrative costs of perfectly detailed control may be much higher than the cost of some margin of individual variability and choice.

Between the minimum and maximum, what will determine the degree of economic control exerted by a state organization? Obviously, the major variable is ideological, as is most vividly illustrated by the extreme positions of the single encompassing socialist state, and of the limited state in a "pluralistic" society providing wide areas of functional autonomy to economic or other organizations.

Even where the ideology of a pluralistic society prevails, however, the factual role of the state is substantially above the minimum. This is especially true in countries seeking rapid economic development and willing to use the power of the state to foster it.

The "liberal" state is likely to intervene in economic organization and policy for a number of fairly standard reasons. For military and defense production, the role of the state is paramount. In addition, the state often intervenes to redress balances, either cross-sectional or temporal. Thus, the state will try to reduce or eliminate sharp fluctuations in the level of economic activity, but also to reduce or prevent inequities in competitive positions or income distributions. Where centralized economic planning is a prominent feature of economic policy, the balance and sequence of economic activities are partly guided by national, aggregative considerations, and not entrusted to the preferences of managers or investors. Similarly, in any economic system—and especially in one undergoing rapid development—the government tends to intervene to break bottlenecks if private action is unable or unlikely to do so. The more functionally interdependent the economy, the greater the potential number and strategic importance of such bottlenecks.

These considerations help to account for the trend for the role of government to expand in all industrial societies—to expand absolutely, if not relative to the growth in complexity of all other aspects of the societies. More generally, the state is essentially the "residuary legatee" of unsolved social problems; regardless of political ideology, it will sooner or later intervene if private solutions are not forthcoming. Cynical critics of state expansion are approximately correct in alleging that, except for some clearly identified "emergency" measures, a function taken on by the government is rarely released.

The probability of increased political participation in industrializing societies has been noted previously. But it is not possible to say that industrialization inevitably engenders "representative government"—or, at least, to get any agreement, across ideological lines, about the essential structure of representative government.[24] The probability of increased nationalism has also been noted. Emotional adherence to national policies may serve to gloss over strains involved in rapid transformation, conflicting interests, and the substantial cultural diversity within some states.

Clearly, the increasing similarity of the technology and even of the organization of production has, if anything, a *negative* relation to political and ideological rapprochement. Industry provides weapons for external war and internal terror. It has not yet produced substantial and reliable restraints on their use.

[24] See Karl de Schweinitz Jr., *Industrialization and Democracy: Economic Necessities and Political Possibilities* (New York: Free Press of Glencoe, Inc., 1964).

Industrial revolutions undoubtedly have their greatest relative impact on other aspects of social organization at early stages of economic transformation. It is then that inconsistent elements of the preindustrial organization of life are shaken and destroyed, and new and necessary forms of social existence are created. Yet some of the explosives planted early carry long fuses, and their effects appear decades or generations after the beginnings of industrialization. This is true of occupational specialization, for example, and particularly the multiplication of highly technical skills. It is not possible to say, however, when an industrial revolution is complete. Industrial revolutions do not have a finite term; they are "permanent." [1] Problems of synchronization and sequence, of consistency and balance continue to vex all industrial societies, and that is the unavoidable prospect of those developing areas that succeed in revamping their economic system.

Before-and-after comparisons have served us moderately well in identifying major types of structural changes in the process of industrialization. But further use of that conceptual model is likely to have limited value in terms of either general propositions or, especially, practical plans. The lack of a stationary state as a destination for

[1] See Arnold S. Feldman and Wilbert E. Moore, "Moot Points in the Theory," in Moore and Feldman, eds., *Labor Commitment and Social Change in Developing Areas* (New York: Social Science Research Council, 1960), Chap. 20, esp. p. 368.

CHAPTER SIX

# The Future of Industrial Societies

industrialization must be added to lack of exact knowledge on rates and sequences as limiting the utility of static comparisons.

In view of our ignorance of the paths to the present and the certainty of continuous change in the future, it may appear rash indeed to attempt to predict the shape of things to come. The problem is further compounded by the circumstance that new variants in structural combinations are more likely to appear than that uniformity will eventually emerge. We may, however, detect directions if not destinations, and perceive processes if not products.

## THE CLOUDED CRYSTAL BALL

The principles of sociology, the propositions and theorems that formalize the relations among social variables, are mainly composed of generalizations that are cross-sectional in character.[2] At whatever level of generality—say, differential delinquency of contemporary American rural high-school dropouts or the universality of the nuclear family—these principles provide static predictability in the classic form: *if* (an independent variable), *then* (a dependent variable). Some available generalizations, however, involve sequential relations, with or without precise timing, and with or without the allegation that the later condition is caused by the earlier one. We have noted, for example, that in the course of modernization death rates fall before birth rates, as the two phenomena are unequally sensitive to the effects of modernization, taken as a global variable. Some unknown portion of the explanation of the eventual or prospective decline in fertility may be attributed to the influence of declining mortality in providing conspicuously higher survival rates of children, but other conditions and motivational elements are certainly involved.

Causal explanation is not essential for temporal prediction if sequences are invariant, but attention to mechanisms is important when relevant conditions are subject to variation, and also for linking isolated predictions into more meaningful systems of explanation.

The art of prophecy, if it is to rest on scientific procedures rather than supernatural inspiration, requires some rather well-machined parts put together in a sensible order. To foretell the future, we should want first to identify probably *persistent* components of the present. Neither the impression of total flux, which may arise from rapid and extensive change, nor the allegation that there are universal "lags" or continuities, has much

2 This section has been adapted from Wilbert E. Moore, "Predicting Discontinuities in Social Change," *American Sociological Review*, 29 (June 1964), 331-38, particularly from p. 332.

validity. It may be true that affective commitments are less likely to change than merely instrumental arrangements, that values are less volatile than the means for their attainment, that supernatural beliefs hold constant while worldly perceptions change. Yet contrary cases are not difficult to find, and a probability matrix by cultural categories has yet to be constructed. Prophecy, in fact, is surest on the basis of extensive stipulation of the present and past, and on a less grand scale than man's total experience. This is not to deny the reality or utility of conceptions of social evolution; it is only a question of the desired detail, and the detail we are looking for cannot be derived deductively from so general a formula. A major difficulty with evolutionary theory—with its component processes of variability, selective adaptation, and partially cumulative change—is that it lacks predictive bite.

For smaller-scale but empirically richer forecasting, three other components of change are useful. For particular societies, or groups of societies having critically relevant common features, one would take account of: *continuation of orderly trends*—for example, rising rates of school enrollment, or the shift of labor force out of agriculture in the course of economic modernization; *planning*—the extensive use of deliberate change in all industrial societies and those attempting to join the group; and *recapitulated experience*—the partial repetition of historic trends, a valuable aid to prognosis of the social change that can be expected in newly developing countries as we have seen.

Any prediction rests upon certain assumptions. Two important ones must be noted here, as neither has a perfect probability. The first assumption is common to all predictions: that there will be a measure of order in that portion of the universe under scrutiny. The interdependence of social actions and organizations validates the conceptual use of *systems,* a notion that informs the social sciences generally. If chaos rules, prophecy cannot, nor for that matter, can man survive. Social survival is the second assumption. It has a special uncertainty: the reliable techniques for total human destruction now at hand. The apostles of apocalypse and the armorers of Armageddon are somewhat persuasive, but we shall assume away oblivion along with chaos, for either would make merely scholarly pursuits unconscionably frivolous.

## THE PROSPECTS FOR ORDERLY CHANGE

Envisioning the indefinite future would be a meaningless enterprise. If, however, we consider the near future to be the remainder of the twentieth century or a little more, the prospects for peering through the inevitable haze are much brighter.

For countries now industrialized we may expect considerable persistence of characteristic features, including such persistent differences as language and everyday customs, political ideologies and perhaps major elements in internal legal systems and power distributions. This is not to say that there will be no changes, but only that they are likely to be gradual and scarcely fundamental. Perhaps more significantly, many of the processes of change identified as part of the sweep of modernization are characteristic also of economically advanced countries. Urbanization, for example, is continuing in all major parts of the world, as are occupational specialization and the organization of specialists into coordinated units—a process we have called bureaucratization.

An interesting question arises, which may be put in a general form: What are the limits to the extrapolation of trends? Clearly, if the "transitional" population growth were to continue at so rapid a rate, limits on economic support would become increasingly evident, and eventually, of course, the plain problem of space would become paramount. Likewise, the transfer of workers out of agriculture could not be complete short of the "automated farm," but extensive mechanization of production and ready transportation for producers might make total urbanization possible. On the basis of experience so far, it appears that mortality rates decline more slowly as the average expectation of life at birth nears the biblical three score years and ten. The theoretical upper limit on occupational specialization would presumably be a distinct occupation for each member of the labor force, but the costs of transportation, exchange, and administrative coordination would certainly become prohibitive well before that point. The limits on secularization have not been fully tested, but there is little basis for believing that man will ever be prepared for life in a purely rational state, without suprarational beliefs that give meaning to human existence, or without emotional ties to others who provide reciprocal affection.

It is in "playing out the string," the pressing of trends to their limits, that industrial societies may achieve a greater congruence than in the more conventional ways of viewing similarities, namely, in social organization and institutions. Not that trends have no structural implications, but those implications are not highly and precisely determinate of social practices.

But let us revert to matters political, for they are likely to be crucial. We have noted that on the record so far there is no necessary correspondence between industrialization and constitutional democracy, and certainly no assurance of international peace. In terms of political dispositions within national states, we have called attention to the likelihood of broadened political participation in the course of economic modernization, and there is some reason to expect increasing formalization of legitimate choice on issues and representatives, within a constitutional framework of legality. The sovereign state, however, is becoming obsolete, particularly in the era that "affords" arsenals of ultimate weapons. Whether some combination of evolutionary experience and purposeful planning will provide methods of international tension-management cannot be predicted with realistic confidence. That issue will be settled well before our target date of the end of the century. Failing a solution, the impact of industry will be a succession of loud bangs, and the end of man.

Abegglen, James C., 51
Adler, John H., 24
Administration, 47, 56-60, 107-8
Africa, 25, 31, 37, 38, 39, 52, 53, 58-59,
    62, 67, 77, 78, 81, 96
Age (see Demographic factors)
Agriculture, 29, 30, 31, 62-64
Aitken, Hugh G. J., 20, 36
Anderson, C. Arnold, 20, 98
Argentina, 77
Asia, 31, 53
Associations, 102-6
Attitudes (see Motives)
Authority, in work organizations, 52-54,
    56-57, 59-60
Automation (see Mechanization)
Autonomous variability, 84

Bauer, Raymond A., 10
Becker, Gary S., 75
Belgium, 25
Birth rates, 48, 73-76
Blumer, Herbert, 12
Bowman, Mary Jean, 100
Braibanti, Ralph, 22, 34, 35
Bureaucracy, 56-61, 107, 113

Capital, as factor in growth, 24-28, 31,
    67-69
Capitalism, 9, 67-68, 70, 93
Catholicism, 35
Change, institutionalized, 32-33
China, 7, 42, 58, 62, 77
Christianity, 34, 96
Clark, Colin, 64
Commitment, 11, 38, 40-41, 50, 60, 104
Communication, 27-28, 34, 57, 100-102
Communism (see Socialist regimes)
Community, 89-92
Consumption, 27, 31, 71-72 (see also In-
    come)
Contraception, 73-76
Culture, of industrial societies, 9-14 (see
    also Industrial societies)

Davis, Kingsley, 73, 85
Death rates, 73-76, 113
Democracy, 109, 113-14


**INDEX**

Demographic factors, 72-80, 82
Denmark, 7, 25, 63
de Schweinitz, Karl, Jr., 36, 109
Disorganization, 89, 90, 91-92
Distribution (see Exchange; Income)

Economic development, defined, 5, 31,
    36
Economic growth, defined, 5, 22
Education, 20, 31, 32, 34, 41, 42-43, 60,
    66-67, 76, 88, 98-100
Encomienda, 29
Engel, Ernest, 71
England, 73
Entrepreneurship, 28-29, 31, 33, 41
Europe, 24
Evolution, 112, 114
Exchange, 31, 40, 42, 43, 62-63, 69-71

Family, 48, 58, 73-75, 86-90 (see also
    Kinship)
Faris, Robert E. L., 14
Feldman, Arnold S., 10, 11, 13, 16, 31,
    36, 41, 51, 52, 87, 92, 110
Fertility (see Birth rates)
France, 73, 80
Functional equilibrium model, 16, 19-20
    (see also System)

Ginsburg, Norton, 24
Goodenough, Ward Hunt, 81
Grauman, John V., 75
Guest, Robert H., 50

Hacienda system, 29
Hagen, Everett E., 41-42
Handicraft production, 30, 64
Harbison, Frederick, 31, 52, 58
Hartshorne, Richard, 24
Harwitz, Mitchell, 38, 52
Hauser, Philip M., 81
Herskovitz, Melville J., 11, 12, 38, 52
Hinduism, 35 (see also India)
History:
    as basis for prediction, 112
    as source of divergence, 17-18
Holton, Richard H., 31, 40
Hong Kong, 25
Hoselitz, Bert F., 20, 34, 37, 41, 46, 71,
    83, 87

Ideology, 34-37